# SIGNS
## FROM PETS IN THE
## AFTERLIFE

### Identifying Messages From
### Pets in Heaven

# SIGNS FROM PETS IN THE AFTERLIFE

## Identifying Messages From Pets in Heaven

# Lyn Ragan

Lyn Ragan
ATLANTA, GA

### Signs From Pets In The Afterlife
*Identifying Gifts from Pets in Heaven*

Book and Cover Design by *Lynn M. Oney*
Cover Photo © Denise Purrington, *All Dogs Go To Heaven*
Edited by Marley Gibson

**Trade paper ISBN** 978-0-9916414-2-0
**e-Book ISBN** 978-0-9916414-3-7

Any Internet references contained in the work are current at publication time, but Lyn Ragan cannot guarantee that a specific location will continue to be maintained.

**Library of Congress Control Number:** 2015919139

**Lyn Ragan**
Atlanta, GA
info@lynragan.com
**www.LynRagan.com**

Printed in the United States of America

This book is dedicated to our precious Pets in Heaven.
Thank you, Sweet Ones, for sharing
your incredible gifts—
Your undying *Love*

# Other Books by Lyn Ragan

**WAKE ME UP! A True Story**
Love and The Afterlife
*fb/WakeMeUpBook*


**WE NEED TO TALK**
Living With The Afterlife
*fb/WeNeedToTalkBook*


**SIGNS FROM THE AFTERLIFE**
Identifying Gifts From The Other Side
*fb/SignsFromTheAfterlife*


**BERC'S Inner Voice**
*(A Children's Book)*
Author, Lyn Ragan
Illustrator, Alison Meyer
*fb/BercsInnerVoice*

# Table of Contents

# Contents Continued

# Introduction

*Until one has loved an animal, a part of one's soul
remains unawakened. ~Anatole France*

P eople often ask if our departed animals know where we
are or if they can find us if we move. The answer is, yes,
to both. Just like our human loved ones who have passed, our
pets in spirit know all, see all, and hear all. They are always
with us, but now they're in a different form—their spirit body.

For many of us, our pets are our children and have become
a very important part of our families. They ask for nothing
from us, yet they somehow present us with a type of love that
can only be described as *unconditional*.

From the perspective of a pet parent, losing a beloved
companion is no different than losing a human child. In some
instances, it can be even more difficult because the guardian is
the primary caregiver and a pet child relies solely upon them
for everything it needs.

Added to that, our society doesn't recognize pets as equals
to human children. Therefore, the loss of a pet will not be
treated with the same kind of compassion or empathy as a
human loss. The grief cycle begins with very little help from
family or friends.

When our pets transition to the other side, they are linked to us through the love that we share with them. **Love** is a very powerful energy that bonds humans and animals. Whether our pets are here on earth or in another dimension, the *energy of love* cannot be broken. Ever.

What signs can I look for from my deceased pet? This is a question many of us ask ourselves. Much like the communications we receive from loved ones who have passed, our pets too, can connect with us through signs and messages.

Our animals will connect in many of the same ways they did while they were in their physical bodies—through dreams, signs, symbols, and physical or non-physical touch. Their desire to communicate with us is no different from that of our human loved ones on the other side.

Our pets, and loved ones, really do want us to know they are okay, safe, and happy. Without question, they want us to know how much we are loved from the afterworld.

The most important key to receiving and acknowledging a gift from your pet in spirit is to have an open mind and a very open heart. There are no rules when it comes to what signs are shared from the other side. If you can think it, so can they. If you can imagine it, so can they. Our fur-kids are uninhibited by a physical body and can be in many places at the same time. A part of them is always with us and can see everything we do, and hear everything we say.

As they watch us grow in our spiritual enlightenment and see us learning more about their new life on the other side, they are all too happy to help us to identify their gifts from the afterworld. For example—if they're sitting beside you when you discover that the butterfly symbolizes their new transition, they may very well send one to cross your path the next time you are paying attention.

If we get excited about studying their new language, (signs and messages-- aka *Spirit Language*), they are over-the-moon thrilled, too. This process is recognized as a graduation. They teach from the other side, and we learn from the earthly plane.

Since we are human, oftentimes all we want is that one big sign that slaps us in the face. That one huge message that says, "Hey, I'm right here." However, when we think we don't get it, we tend to believe our pets and loved ones have left us for good. That is so far from the truth.

As with any relationship we share here on earth, it also takes great effort and dedication to continue our connections with our pets in spirit. They can't possibly do all of the work, and frankly, we're kidding ourselves if we think they should.

It takes two—*Spirit and You.*

Retraining our minds requires effort and a lot of practice, but it can pay us back with priceless dividends. If you've never experienced the wonder and the mystery of receiving miraculous signs and signals from the spiritual realm, please consider giving it a try. All you need is a heightened sense of awareness and an increased consciousness.

Messages from your loyal companions can potentially be life changing when they are identified. Most often, they are subtle signs, but even the slightest ones are communications that can speak the loudest. Any sign or signal from the spiritual realm is an *important* one and each has a very specific *purpose* designated for the individual recipient.

Sometimes the signs appear to comfort us in times of sadness and deep grief. In other circumstances, they are guideposts or traffic lights to direct us along our life path. Either way, it is our divine right to accept the gifts from our spirit family and this does include our adoring pets, too.

*It truly is a skill that any of us can develop.*

It does not require us to be psychic or to have mediumistic abilities, although we were all born with these very gifts. All we need is a bit of faith and a lot of trust in our much-loved pets. We already love them completely, so trusting them in their pure unadulterated spirit form should be effortless.

So what signs do we look for? The best way to notice them is to become aware that they exist. It certainly can't hurt to observe the small wonders that are happening around you every day. For example, on your drive to work one day you see a raccoon on the side of the road. Did you know a raccoon can deliver a spiritual message?

*The Raccoon reminds us to look at the whole picture. The seen and the unseen.* Not only that, if that raccoon grabbed your attention from out of nowhere, this could be a sign from your pet in heaven saying, "It's me, I'm right here with you."

Because symbolic signs are unique and very individual, they may not always be easily recognized or immediately understood. From birds, animals, people, places, things, or events, symbolic signs are presented in **many** forms and are quite simply, the messenger; *the messenger of spirit*.

Many look at Afterlife Signs as proof of a Hereafter. However, what constitutes proof? Evidence of an afterlife is a very personal matter. What is undeniable validation for one person may carry no weight for another.

**Proof must come from within.**

Yet proof, can often appear upon the hands of knowledge. Moreover, knowledge is something we all seek to find.

When I decided to write this book with pets in mind, I had to appreciate that many of the signs we recognize from our loved ones on the other side are **exactly** the same as those from our beloved pets. The information shared here is based solely on my education and personal experiences with my special ones in the afterlife. My intention is not to persuade you to believe what I have come to know as my personal truths. Rather, I wish only to share the possibilities to help assist you in your journey in identifying signs from *your* pets in Spirit.

The list of afterlife signs is truly endless and is not limited to the few listed in this book. Those that are documented are the more popular ones that thousands of people enjoy, recognize, and acknowledge. Because they are often seen and documented, our pets in spirit know this all too well. They will conspire to use ANY tool they can to capture our attention. As our relationships continue to grow with our departed pets, the signs they share will also change form as we educate ourselves.

It is important for us to keep our expectations simple. Our signs will show up in ways that complement our lifestyle. Please remember there is no *one sign that fits all* scenarios, and there are **no rules** for how they appear. The message is always clear and direct though—*I love you*—and no sign or message is ever intended to frighten or mislead you. Always try to remember that fear is an emotion, and one that Hollywood has perfected tapping into.

*The only thing we have to fear is fear itself.* ~FDR

It is important for us to show our gratitude to our pets in heaven. We need to be thankful for every sign or message we receive, and express that thanks verbally or from within. Our adored pets know all, see all, and hear all now... so saying "thank you" is one of the easiest things we can do.

When we die, we simply move from this world directly into the next one. The only thing we lose is our physical vessel, our bodies. Our personality and the love we carry for those we left behind, stays with us. In spirit, we literally have the best of both worlds: this dimension and the spirit world.

Do we hold our pets or loved ones back by continuing our relationships through signs and messages? Absolutely not! Our human minds have no way to digest, or wrap around the depth of the life in spirit. Their strength, agility, and power are greater than *anything* we can possibly imagine. In energy form, aka spirit form, they can be, and are, in more than one place at the same time. They can be here with us at the very same moment they are working, playing, or even visiting another loved one.

So no, we can never, **ever**, hold them back.

Lastly, the bottom line is that our spirit family and our pets really do want us to know they are okay. In addition, they want us to be okay, too. Their biggest wish is for their family and friends on earth, to live a happy and joyful life.

Knowing our relationships can continue past this physical life is a very big blessing and a wonderful gift, as well. Everything may happen for a reason, but sometimes a change in perspective can help us to see what we have gained... not what we've lost.

# Part One

## Sensing Our Pets in Spirit

# Bedroom Visitations

*There are no mistakes, no coincidences. All events are*
*blessings given to us to learn from. ~Elizabeth Kubler-Ross*

D espite the fact that sensing a deceased pet is a common
experience, it is seldom talked about. Like grief, it's
more comfortable for most to deny it rather than to speak about
it. Even reality is no match for love.

Sensing a deceased pet is a true spiritual gift.

There are all sorts of visions and images that can occur
along our divine journeys. Some people see future events,
some hear voices in their head, and others will encounter lights
or images of special forms. The most common type of contact
from a deceased pet is *sensing* their presence.

Especially in the bedroom.

Have you ever been lying in bed, waking up or falling
asleep, when you felt movement next to you? As soon as you
opened your eyes to see who or what it was though, you were
left with nothing but wonderment or sudden confusion. You
might have thought, "Did I just make that up? Did I really feel
my sweet pet hop on the bed?"

Whether they are seen in apparitions or in dreams, or not
at all, our beloved pets continue to live in our hearts and minds.
For some, however, they continue to linger in our senses
through sight, sound, smell, touch, and indeed, physical

presence. For many, it's quite clear… our pets stay with us.

Sensing the presence of a deceased pet is a very normal occurrence, but it is rarely discussed. Fearing being labeled crazy or possibly considered insane, most who experience this phenomenon will hold it close like a treasured secret, instead of sharing it aloud.

Feeling the existence of the Afterlife is more the norm rather than the exception. Studies have shown that over eighty percent (80%) of us have experienced visions of departed loved ones and/or pets within one month after their death. Almost half reported interacting with them.

It is quite common for us to feel our deceased pet jump up on, walk across, or even lie down on the bed. Our human eyes may not see them anywhere, yet we know for certain we felt the depression of the mattress. Without a doubt, it felt no different than when they were here in their physical form. Much like what Marley experienced only hours after her dog passed away.

*When I was twelve-years-old, my dog, Candy, got run over. She lived at our farm and had never been inside our house, let alone, my bedroom. The night she died, she came into my room and stood on her back paws with the front one on my bed. She told me she was okay and she thanked me for taking her in when she was a puppy and being her friend. She said she would miss me and then she turned and left the room. I remember it being a dream back then, but the more I'm involved in the paranormal, I realize she was really coming to thank me. What a moment! ~Marley B, Savannah, Georgia.*

**It is normal** to feel our pet sitting or lying in the bed beside us. Our fur-kids have the ability to manifest the *sense of their physical contact* without actually touching us, hence feeling the movement of the mattress.

Many people might discount the occurrence thinking they've imagined it, or somehow made it up. Yet it is a distinct feeling and a complete *knowing* unlike any other, when spirit is near. We might also see an apparition, a colored light, an outline of their body, a transparent mist, or we may see nothing at all. Yet, the *feeling* that a much-loved pet is close, even ones you think you don't know, **is** and always will be, very real. Much like what Rickie experienced when she was awakened in the middle of the night by movement.

*I was sleeping in the spare bedroom since my husband was sick with a cold and flu. I was in a deep sleep when, all of a sudden, I felt something jump onto the foot of my bed. That startled me awake. I laid there for a while and then looked over at the clock; it was 2:00 o'clock in the morning.*

*The blanket by my feet started moving and it felt like little feet were walking around. I could FEEL the blanket being pressed in, almost like a cat would do. I thought, "Darn, that feels like a cat. Wait, we don't have a cat."*

*After getting up and going to the bathroom, I snuggled back in after seeing there was **no** cat on the bed. Once again, something really small and lightweight started walking around-- on top of the blanket at my feet. I started pinching myself to make sure I was awake. I was very puzzled and wondered what was going on.*

*A few minutes later the cat moved around more, trying to find the right spot to snuggle up. It finally curled up right by my foot. There was nothing I could do but accept that a cat was with me in my bed. ~Rickie F., Jacksonville, Florida.*

**Some of us** will feel *goose bumps* when our pets are next to us. When spirit touches us, it can feel as real as physical contact. Sometimes they enjoy running their energy through our hair and when this happens, it feels like little bugs crawling around on top of our head.

Many experience ringing in their ears. Audible or verbal communication may take place as well, but we must keep in mind that every experience is different. As unique as our DNA is, so too are the communications from the afterworld.

No two people will experience the same thing.

Take Teresa for example. She was surprised to feel her cat so close to home after she passed.

*For sixteen and a half years, Furball was a pleasure to be around. It is a delight to know she is never far away. I still feel her walking around on my bed in the mornings. Love is the bridge that keeps her in my heart so fondly. ~Teresa C., Calgary, Alberta (Canada)*

**Our pets allow** us to feel their presence in order to teach us, and validate for us, that physical death is not the end of who we are. They also teach us that it is possible to continue to build our relationships. Much like Janet's experience. When her fur-baby passed away, she never imagined he could share his presence in such a memorable way.

*Cooper had a brain tumor and had to be put down last July. I was devastated and cried for days and days. He was my constant companion and went everywhere with me. He slept with me, was always near, and even barked at me when he thought I should go to bed at night.*

*One evening lying in bed, I was "talking" to him, crying, and missing him so much. I felt him jump on the bed and I felt him walk toward me...the mattress actually moved. Then, I smelled him and instantly knew he was there. It brought a sense of peace over me that words can't begin to describe. ~Janet M., Lafayette, Indiana.*

**Our pets share** with us that the love we hold dear and close does go with them to the other side. Through signs, messages, and sensing their presence, they let us know their love for us continues. A perfect example of this *love* came when Helen least expected it.

*Max, my handsome Rottweiler, lived a long and happy life. His spirit had always been remarkably joyful, but his sixteen-year-old body couldn't keep up. I missed him terribly yet I knew he had to be healthy and happy where he was. Max's love for me was larger than life—he was in a league all his own.*

*A few weeks after his passing, I decided to nap one afternoon. Max's brother, Troy, was fast asleep beside me. Thirty minutes or so later, I felt Troy stand up on the bed, walk across my legs, and jump down to the floor. I wasn't ready to get up so I hollered at him, "Troy, get your butt back in bed."*

*I listened to his nametag dangle against his collar while he left the bedroom and then headed down the hallway. Refusing to open my eyes, I shouted at him again to get back in bed, but now I was wide-awake and a tad irritated, too. I propped up on my elbows and when I did, Troy lifted his head from the bed and gave me a look like I had lost my mind.*

*It took a minute to realize we weren't alone. That wasn't Troy who jumped off the bed, it was Max. What a wonderful comfort knowing he's still here and still resting in bed with me and his brother. ~Helen B., Tucson, Arizona.*

**Another beautiful example** of continued love from the other side came when Judy heard from her deceased cats.

*Eddie was thirteen-years-old when he passed in 2003. His favorite spot in the house was in our bed and between our heads. He would lie there peacefully and purr up a storm. We always told him, "Purr us to sleep, Eddie." After he passed, I would wake in the middle of the night because I could hear his loud purr or his noisy meow. We had no other cats in the house. I knew Eddie was letting me know he was still with me.*

*A few months after Eddie's death, we welcomed a new cat named, Ginger. She became our pampered princess. Four years later, Ginger became very ill and we lost her, too. The last few months of her life, I had to keep her in a crate at night beside my bed for her safety. She got very tired of the crate and would pull on the lock all night long. It made a very loud clanking noise. After Ginger passed, we put everything away. Yet every night thereafter, I would still hear Ginger beside my bed pulling on the door of her crate. Clank, clank, clank. Her presence was very strong. ~Judy S., Orlando, Florida.*

**Sensing our pets** or feeling their presence is solid assurance of an endless love. The kind of love that can only be measured with *infinite divinity*.

# A Soul's Love

*The soul is the same in all living creatures,*
*although the body of each is different. ~Hippocrates*

Have you ever felt a gentle paw rest upon your shoulder, but when you turned to inspect, nothing was there? Maybe you felt the rub of a cat across your leg, but when you looked down, there was no cat to be seen?

You didn't make this up and no, you are not crazy. Each one of us experiences a unique sensation when a deceased pet is present. In the days following their passing, it is quite normal to feel a brush against your leg, to sense your hand being nudged, to experience a gentle touch, to hear them walking or running through the house, or to get a tingle on the top of your head—their energy running through your hair.

The presence of our deceased pets often feels very comforting and peaceful. For many, this is the very reason their presence is dismissed – because it feels too good. In addition, for others, the focus is on how scary it is, which causes the connection to be missed, broken, or misinterpreted.

Feeling the caress of Spirit right after their passing is common, yes, but what many don't realize is that our pets keep visiting long after their death; for years in fact. They show us their continued survival in many forms, and sensing them still near is a strong reminder of how close they are.

Their deepest wish is to console our grief and bestow upon us the most valuable knowledge of all—that *life continues past death* and *love lives forever*. Regina learned this the hard way after a most rewarding experience.

*Andy, my fifteen-year-old Yorkshire Terrier, passed away two years ago of lung complications. Four months later, my husband died. If it weren't for Coco, my then thirteen-year-old Chihuahua, I don't know what I would have done.*

*One afternoon I thought I had lost Coco and after an hour-long search for her, I started to lose my mind. I stood in my kitchen and cried when I heard the front door open and close. I peeked around the corner to see who it could be, but there was no one there. From out of nowhere, I heard the faint sound of a tag dangling against the metal of a collar. It sounded exactly like Andy's collar and in that moment, I also felt something brush against my legs. I then heard the tapping of little feet walking into the breakfast room, and in shock, I followed the sound as it led me to a closet where I kept dog food and treats. When I approached the sliding door, a faint bark could be heard and right away, I knew it was my darling, Andy. I opened the door and sitting there, was Coco.*

*In all of my screams and frantic calls for her, she never made a sound. I was never so pleased to see her. Andy's continued love and support from the other side is honestly, quite indescribable. ~Regina B., Shelby, Virginia.*

**We are our** pets Heaven and just because their physical body is no longer alive, it doesn't mean their soul loves us any less. We are loved from beyond, and always will be.

# Knock, Knock, Knock

*Venture outside your comfort zone.*
*The rewards are worth it. ~Rapunzel*

S ome signs are often ones that cannot be ignored. Have you found yourself watching the television, or talking on the telephone, when suddenly you hear knocking on the counter in the kitchen?

Maybe your other dogs started to bark and ran to the sound excitedly, but once you arrived to explore there was no logical reason for the loud knocks? At this point, there was nothing you could do but scratch your head. At least until it happened a second time, or even a third. One thing you knew for sure, everyone heard the knocks at the same time.

Have you ever found yourself lying on the sofa or in bed about to fall asleep when out of nowhere, you heard three distinct knocks on the wall, or on the door, or against the window? Has this happened more than one time?

After looking for a rational cause, you may have noticed the knocks occurred at a particular time. For you, the hour may be significant. It could be the time your pet passed on. This isn't always the case, however.

One thing is for certain, the knocks were loud, clear, and you know they happened. Once you receive this type of sign, time and time again, you will begin to understand that it is a big message from your trusted companion. There will be no one who will convince you otherwise. The loud sounds can and probably will continue for quite some time. Especially after your pet understands you value this unique sign from them.

Beloved pets are often very eager, if not extremely excited, to let us know they are still a part of our lives. Receiving a symbolic message, a sign, a coincidence, or a synchronistic event, is very comforting and a blessing all at the same time.

While several people can feel their pets near and watching over them, there are many who find this perception very difficult to understand. They can't be sure that what they felt was actually what they thought it was. This causes doubt to creep in and the entire message can be dismissed as a *figment of their imagination*. For Penny, it took more than one occurrence before she understood her message.

*Polly, my Golden Retriever, was a dream dog. It broke my heart when she passed suddenly at the age of ten. The day after her death, my three dogs and I snuggled up on the sofa to watch TV. A few minutes went by when out of nowhere, three very loud knocks came from the front door. The boys shot up off the sofa, barking loudly. There was no one there when I answered. I failed to put two and two together until it happened again the next day. Again the day after that. Our sweet Polly was telling us she was still a part of our family, only she was in a different form now. What a wonderful gift to know this. ~Penny W., Ethel, Mississippi.*

**Love isn't always** a silent whisper from the Afterlife. Sometimes it can be very loud… and unforgettable.

# Moving Objects

*Whoever said that diamonds are a girl's best friend...
never owned a dog ~Author Unknown*

This method of Afterlife communication, *moving objects*, is commonly used on those whose attention is the hardest to gain. Even when it's obvious that something has been changed, moved, or relocated, we might still find ourselves dismissing the amazing statement behind the sign—*I'm here*.

Have you gone to grab your keys from where you always placed them, religiously, but they weren't there when you went to leave? You had to start a search for several minutes, if not days, when you finally located them in a planter outside on the patio. You might have asked yourself, "What the heck? How'd they get there? Did I unconsciously put them in the dirt and don't remember?" No, you did not put your keys in the planter; your darling pet did.

They wanted your attention, and now, they have it.

Sometimes our sweet pets move objects to get our attention. Things that mean something to us, or to them, can be repositioned strategically to make us seek and find the article in question.

A few common items might be toys, bones, bows, pictures, keys, eyeglasses, jewelry, money, cards, magazines, remote controls, and paper products. Whatever the object is, if our pet knows we will notice the item missing at some point, it is precisely what they will choose. Let's take a look at Diane's cat as a perfect example for getting attention.

*Three months after Amber's death came December 2012 with no snow on the books. A few days before Christmas, I grabbed my jacket from the closet (the one I always wore outside), and went into the garage to grab some Kleenex. I was headed to her gravesite behind the barn and knew I would cry.*

*Upon reaching into my pocket to place the Kleenex, I noticed it was wet and very cold. I then pulled out a handful of ice. This wasn't the regular kind of ice. This ice looked as though someone had placed a snowball in my pocket and then took it out. All that was left was sitting in my hand. Staring at the few pieces lying in plain sight, I shouted, "What the heck is this!"*

*I put the ice in the sink and headed outside to Amber's grave. By the time I arrived, it hit me. I had JUST asked her to show me a sign that she was still here. There it was. I raced back to the garage, but the ice had already melted. My pocket was still wet, but there was no ice. I pulled out the Kleenex and put them in a safe place to remember her by. What a beautiful gift from my precious cat, Amber. I miss her so. ~Diane B., Macedon, New York.*

**Maybe you have** a photograph of your pet that keeps falling. Perhaps you've noticed one of their toys keeps appearing even after you've put it up. Did you really place that wrapper on the coffee table after you had already thrown it in the garbage can? When did you start turning off the mouse to your computer or laptop?

If your pet loved to play on the earthly plane, it's most likely they'll thoroughly enjoy playing with you when they get to the other side. Our physical bodies may not go with us when we transition, but our personalities certainly do. A perfect example of a pet's personality surviving death comes from Betty's story. Her cat loves to play with her.

*Trip was a Bombay cat and a true angel. We spent eighteen amazing years together. He wasn't just a cat. He was my best friend and the smartest cat I have ever seen.*

*A week after he passed away, I started noticing things not being where I swore I had left them. Things like my keys, my eyeglasses, my writing pen, and even my phone. I really thought I was starting to lose my grip on life.*

*One afternoon I was reading a book when from the corner of my eye, I saw one of Trip's balls roll across the floor and then stop at my feet. At first, it scared the daylights out of me, but then I very quickly realized something— I wasn't losing my mind. Rather, it was the action of my little boy reminding me he hadn't left. How lucky am I to have this beautiful being continue to share his love and his cute annoying personality? Very lucky am I! ~Betty B., Jacksonville, Florida.*

**When your pet** wants your attention, they will go to great lengths to master their communication. Even if they have to repeat it several times before you *get it*. Linda's pug is a perfect example of repeated signs. She had to work extra hard to get Linda's attention.

*Lucy was loved by everyone she met. She knew no strangers and that made her very special. My heart felt like it was ripped from my chest when she died. She wasn't just my dog, she was my child and I missed her badly.*

*Lucy had so many toys it wasn't funny. Yet, she played with every single one at one time or another. Her toy box was located in the living room and I couldn't bear to remove it. A couple of days after her death, I found one of her toys on the couch. I figured my husband or my daughter put it there and didn't think too much about it. I simply picked it up and put it back in her toy box, wishing the entire time she was here.*

*I walked into the kitchen to start dinner and sitting on the floor in front of me was another one of Lucy's toys. This time, I questioned the appearance. I was home alone and there was NO way someone else put that toy there. As I leaned over to pick it up, tears falling to the floor, I heard something crash in the family room.*

*I wiped my eyes and went to investigate the unexpected sound. Imagine my shock when I saw Lucy's picture lying on the carpet. I was stunned. There wasn't a doubt in my mind she was here with me, and still is. It really is true—love does live forever. I'm a believer. ~Linda W., Huntsville, Alabama.*

**Let us not** forget that some moving objects will create noise. It's not meant to startle us, even though at times it does. It is only intended to surprise and awaken our awareness.

# 5

# Pennies From Heaven
Pennies | Nickels | Dimes | Quarters

*We have more to learn from animals than animals*
*have to learn from us. ~Anthony Douglas Williams*

T here's an old saying that goes like this... *They say when*
*an angel misses you, they toss a penny down from Heaven.*
Sadly, there's a lot of truth to this adage that many never see or
even experience.

Spirits love to place things in our path over and over again
that are significant to them, or to us. Once we find that first
coin and instinctively know it was sent by our beloved
companion, everything changes. They will start placing
pennies (or the corresponding coin for them) everywhere, so
we can't miss them. Why do they do this?

Because they receive as much happiness and love from it
as we do. They know we identify their sign as a way to
communicate and though it may not be a sloppy kiss, or a soft
meow, it is still an enormous bond of unconditional love.

Spiritual signs are very personal and are designed
especially for us. These messages will always carry a sincere
meaning, no matter how small or insignificant they appear to
be. They are our individual signs and not for the eyes or heart
of another. Dorothy's gift is an individualized example. Even
though she knew she was receiving a sign, it took a few hours

before she learned whom it had come from.

*On June 6, I went out to dinner with some wonderful friends. When the waitress approached with the check, a shiny quarter literally jumped out at me. Immediately, I was reminded of my Uncle Billy. He was such a kind person and always had a pocket filled with shiny quarters to hand out to the kids.*

*At this same moment, a friend had announced the time; it was 4:44 p.m. I was aware that this too was a sign, but couldn't remember its meaning. We continued to chat a bit longer and as we were leaving, my friend asked me the year of the quarter. I looked and saw, 1998. At that time, I had no clue what the year could possibly mean.*

*Four hours later, I received a call from my husband. My precious Pomeranian, Kayla, had passed away. My heart was broken. I knew she had lived a long and happy life, but I couldn't help myself; I cried. Kayla had been with me through good times and bad times. She was my rock.*

*I am thankful to have had my friends present to witness the signs Kayla gave me. Through Uncle Billy, she let me know she was okay when she used that shiny quarter as her sign. The year 1998 is the year she was born.*

*The time 4:44— she was telling me I had nothing to fear. All was as it should be and all was well. She was letting me know I was surrounded by her energy and how she loved me and supported me.*

*Her physical body is gone, but she will never leave me. I will never forget my baby. RIP Kayla. I love you so much!*
*~Dorothy Li, Canton, Georgia*

**The coin may** have great meaning simply by the year it is dated. It might be the year our pet was born, or the year might represent a special celebration or anniversary. Another perfect example of a *penny find* occurred when Nancy discovered she was receiving signs from her Boxer.

*I was smothered in grief when Reba passed away. Twelve wonderful years together didn't feel like enough time together. I cried everyday. Reba was my child, not a dog or companion.*

*The day I received her ashes, I placed her on top of the pillow she slept on beside me. It was the first night I fell asleep since her death. The following morning, I went to pick her up to move her into the living room where she would stay. Much to my astonishment, sitting on top of her urn was a very bright and shiny penny. I stood there, shocked.*

*I'm an old woman and live alone so I knew no one placed it there. It had to have come from Reba. As soon as I realized that, I broke down into tears. What a beautiful gift from my baby girl. She hasn't stopped there. I find pennies all the time. She enjoys reminding me how much she loves me. I always tell her how much I love her too. ~Nancy S., Paradise, California.*

**Whether it's a** penny, a nickel, a dime, or a quarter, coins can be a sign from your deceased pet. They can also be a form of communication from your angels or from your spiritual guides as well.

Sometimes coins can be found in the most unusual places, (sitting on the shelf inside the refrigerator), or when they are least expected, (sitting on the bench beside you). When it happened to Rachel, she couldn't believe it. She had no idea it was possible to communicate with her Labrador in Heaven.

*Hope was a one-of-a-kind girl. Highly trained in*

*obedience and retrieval, she was a very smart dog. We had just received her Therapy Dog Certification papers and I was thrilled that her gift of life would provide happiness for a child in need. Sadly, we were involved in a car accident and she didn't survive her injuries.*

*My life with Hope was a full one, but when she died, everything came to a screeching halt. I missed her, but mostly I missed us. We were a team. As crazy as this may sound, I never, ever, once thought of her dying. Yet there I was, stuck in a dark grief cycle I couldn't dig myself out of.*

*About a week after she died, I was in my kitchen making lunch. I grabbed a loaf of bread and when I did, a dime fell to the floor. I bent down to pick it up, but I had no clue where it came from. I put it on the counter and continued making my food. I opened the refrigerator to get the mayonnaise and when I pulled it out, another dime fell to the floor. I quickly turned to look to see if the first one was still there on the counter; it was. I picked up the second one and this time I stared at it with a little more curiosity.*

*I now have a jar filled with dimes. They may fall or roll, but they always appear at the exact time I need them. Hope... what can I say? I always knew she was a special girl. ~Rachel G., Denver, Colorado.*

**No matter where** we locate our signs, the message is quite clear. Our sweet animals are sharing a very special message… "I am always with you. You never have to worry, because you are never alone."

# 6

# License Plates, Signs, and Billboards

*If I could be half the person my dog is, I'd
be twice the human I am. ~Charles Yu*

S eeing a message, a name, or a specific set of numbers on a license plate can be a direct and very personal sign. For example, while reminiscing about a loved one in the car, you stop at a red light. You look at the license plate on the vehicle in front of you and it reads, *I ♥ Charlie.*

You sit for a moment, stunned, and ask yourself, "Can that be a sign?" You already know it is and now all you have to do is trust it. Your devoted pet has positioned you at the right place at the right time. Yet, **believing** can be a hard thing to do.

Synchronicity plays a big role in our lives. Our pets can make a simultaneous event occur before our very eyes; it's easy for them and it does help them capture our attention. A great example of concurrent messages is told in Denise's story. When she received her first sign, she doubted it. The second one however, changed her mind completely.

*One bright sunny day, my sister and I found ourselves driving to a pet cemetery in Bethlehem, Georgia. The name of the city attracted us. Winding in and out of streets, we came across one called, "Charles Place." Charlie came to mind instantly, but certainly it wasn't a sign from him. Charlie was my first ever dog and was literally, my sidekick. He wasn't just a Chihuahua. He was half-human. An hour later we decided to stop and eat if we found a diner. Just as we said it, a billboard appeared that read, "Charlie's Restaurant". Without question, I knew it was him. I've learned how to look for his signs now. I love how he still loves me. ~Denise O., Ellijay, Georgia.*

**By using synchronicity**, our pets can position us exactly where we need to be. We can be driving along, minding our own business, and haphazardly look over at a large billboard. Our eyes leap across the words, *Thank you 4 loving me.* Or maybe it says, *Surprise! I'm right here!*

Amazingly, we've received a message from the beyond. Sure, thousands of others will read that same billboard too, but none of them experienced *that* message exactly the way that we did. Why? Because we've driven that road a hundred times before, if not more, and not once have we looked at that billboard sign. Our minds have always been somewhere else, focusing on work, life, relationships, children, or other things.

On this day though, our head moved and our eyes glazed over a set of unique words. In that single instant, a new language began to form and in those delicate moments, life started to change.

Our darling pets can and do, share extraordinary messages with us. They're called *gifts of love.* Becky's experience is a great example of a spectacular gift. When Abby waltzed into her life, everything changed.

*On a cold, snowy January morning, I sat down at my computer and as if a magic wand had been waved over me, something made me Google a Minneapolis K-9 rescue website. There sat a dog in her golden years named Abigail, in need of a forever home. Abby joined our family on February 11, 2011, just weeks shy of her thirteenth birthday.*

*After her foster mom shared everything she knew about the dog, she whispered in Abby's ear, "Good-bye Bah Bah." It was a nickname she gave her and soon we realized why. Abby looked like a sweet little lamb after her grooming sessions.*

*It didn't take long for Abby to adjust to life in our home. We knew she loved being a part of our family by the way she danced her special happy dance. Yes, she enjoyed Minnesota life (even the snow) and the great outdoors. Abby could no longer hear and her vision was not the best, but it didn't matter. She was a sweet soul with a zest for life.*

*Little did we know everything was about to change. In November of 2012, Abby's groomer discovered a lump on her neck. Tests confirmed she had squamous cell carcinoma on her tongue. The vet said there was nothing we could do because the cancer had already spread to her lymph nodes.*

*I was not going to give up on Abby so easily. I sought the assistance of an animal communicator and Abby was grateful for their conversation. "I am finishing up on my life's work. Soon it will be complete and I'll be ready to go. I love my new family. They are great teachers and I needed to learn about unconditional love and learn that it would come to me. Thank you for talking to me and giving me a voice," said Abby.*

*In the next eight months, we provided loving care and support to Abby while on her cancer journey. She had sessions at Healing Touch for Animals®, remote healings on her tumor by a local Qigong Master; I invoked the healing power of heavenly angels, and used essential oils and gemstones as well.*

*Abby's tumor had not grown or spread to any other area of her body, but her tongue was beginning to disappear so we fed her by spoon and provided her with a drinking fountain. At a check-up in March, the vet said she honestly thought Abby wouldn't make it to spring, yet there she was.*

*A week before Abby's health took a turn, I awoke and heard, "We can't do anything more." Within days, her tumor spread like wildflowers. In her final animal communication she said, "I am ready when my family is ready." She didn't want to burden us with making the decision on our own.*

*Abby's Angel Day was July 29, 2013. We spent the morning honoring her with her favorite breakfast and sat together outside by the garden— one of her favorite spots. We were flooded with signs. On our final walk as a family, we found a white feather **and** a penny. During our last family gathering around the fire table, we received an angel-flame. In a root beer toast to her at bedtime the night before, a heart formed inside the glass.*

*On what would have been Abby's sixteenth birthday, a car in front of me had a license plate that read, "BAH". There was no mistaking it, this was a sign from her. On **my** first birthday without her, another license plate appeared. It read, "BAA." I love receiving her signs. ~Becky N., Brooklyn Park, Minnesota.*

**Our pets put** everyone and everything exactly where they need to be by using synchronicity as a tool of choice. They send messages and share signs with the utmost of divine love. If their messages could speak, they would clearly say, "Our love can never die."

# 7

# Cloud Formations

*If there comes a day when we can't be together, keep me in your heart—I'll stay there forever. ~Winnie the Pooh*

M any believe the images we see in the clouds foretell what is to come. While others think they give indications of one's current state-of-mind. Whatever it is we believe, one thing is for certain, cloud formations capture the imagination.

Seeing among the clouds the face of a pet, or a beautiful angel, or a loved ones real features, is considered a divine announcement. These signs are not only filled with love, but are prophetic, wise, and also quite mysterious.

Have you ever seen an interesting shape in the clouds? If you have, you're not alone. Clouds can take on shapes and forms of all kinds. Some are obscure while others are quite obvious.

Recognizing cloud images brings about an awareness of positive life affirming guidance from the afterlife. It's difficult at times to wrap our minds around the abilities of our pets in spirit. However, if we can set aside the confusion for a moment and focus on the actual gift given, we can then begin to understand that *love* is all there is. The continued devotion from the other side can indeed remove all of the doubt we live with.

Images in the form of clouds can appear as your dog, as your cat, your bird; just about anything. When Teresa looked up at the sky shortly after her cat passed, we can only imagine her surprise when she witnessed a remarkable portrait.

*Raised from a kitten, my female Tuxedo cat, Furball, was a joy. I had the pleasure of her company for sixteen and a half years. At the end of her life she wasn't doing well, and I had to make that awful decision to let her go back to kitty heaven.*

*It was so hard to have to do. I went home and wrestled with the thoughts of whether or not I made the right choice. As I stood in the kitchen doing dishes, I was prompted to look up at the clouds and when I did, there in a perfect cloud form, was a sitting cat facing toward me.*

*I was so touched. Furball sent me a sign to let me know she was in Heaven. She was safe and sound and that gave me peace of mind. ~Teresa C., Calgary, Alberta (Canada)*

**The Afterlife isn't** as complicated as we've been led to believe. Our pets want to stay connected to us and be in touch. The only hurdle in communicating with the Afterlife is *us*. Either we don't believe in after-worldly connections, we don't know *what* to look for, or we distrust the very signs and messages they send.

*Doubt* is the number one reason messages are missed.

When a sign is wanted or needed, look up into the skies. Study the clouds above you. Ask for a cloud sign, and then give your pet a few minutes to design a cloud formation. You might be very surprised at what you see.

Love is the **key** for keeping us together. Our souls are made of the love we share. These types of personal and timely messages can illuminate our interconnectedness with the other side. Like Mack's communications with his dog in spirit, their connection is a perfect model of Divine Love.

*With me for nearly twelve years, Roofus, my Beagle, suddenly passed away. I came home from work one afternoon to find his lifeless body lying in his bed. Needless to say, my heart was broken and even though I'm an old man, I have no problem admitting I cried a river of tears. I've witnessed several signs since his passing. One afternoon I begged him to let me know he was all right. About thirty minutes later, I walked outside and looked up. Sitting in the sky was a perfect heart painted in the clouds. Almost immediately, I felt an overwhelming sense of happiness and peace race through me. I have no doubt that was my boy telling me he loved me and was still here with me, too. This wasn't the last communication from him either. He enjoys sending me ladybugs and white butterflies on a regular basis. Your daddy loves and misses you, Roofus. ~Mack B., Gilbert, Arizona.*

**When we open** our hearts and minds, we become aware of the energetic pull that attracts our attention. Cloud formations are tailored specifically for each person and for our needs at that very moment. When Becky received a sweet surprise minutes after Abby passed on, she cried with gratitude.

*A local teen composed a song called, "Clouds," while he was traveling on his personal journey with cancer. He passed two weeks before Abby, my senior rescue who too, was dealing with cancer.*

*On Abby's angel day, we played the young teen's song over and over again. It was so uplifting and it kept us positive and strong for our little girl's day. After she passed, I looked up at the sky when I saw a perfect angel wing formed in the clouds. Our baby girl was letting us know she was okay, and had made it home safe and sound. ~Becky N., Brooklyn Park, Minnesota.*

**It is okay** to trust our pets in spirit. They loved us unconditionally when they shared their lives with us, and they will continue to do so until we are reunited with them once again. Our pets enjoy sharing their signs with us. When we actually "see" them, their enthusiasm is increased and they can't wait to do it again. Melissa's experience took her to her knees. She knew what she saw was there, but her mind had a tough time believing it was true.

*I found myself looking up one morning. I didn't normally take the time to do that, but something obviously pulled me to it. I couldn't believe my eyes. In the sky was a perfect cloud in the form of a smiley face. I blinked hard and looked again; it was still there. I fell to my knees and burst into tears.*

*My little Corgi had passed two days earlier. He was buried with his favorite yellow blanket that was covered in smiley faces. I am convinced this was Toby's way of letting me know he was okay in Heaven. I look up quite a bit now, searching for his signs. ~Melissa P., Sparta, Kentucky.*

**When our pets** share a cloud formation as their gift to us, they share an incredible message… "The love we have cannot be measured. Please believe in me and trust that I am with you… always."

# 8

# Dream-Visitations and Visions

*All our dreams can come true, if we have the
courage to pursue them. ~Walt Disney*

Dreaming about pets is a very common experience. Because we're sleeping, we are in that *in between place* that links our earthly bodies to the spirit world.

During sleep, our working minds are not engaged. Things we'd normally stop and discount while awake, such as the appearance of a deceased pet, isn't as important to us while we're in that sleep state. On the contrary, in our sleep world our pets feel more alive than ever before.

Dream-visitations are an ideal place for our pets to make contact. A form of Afterlife connections between us and them, our pets, loved ones, spirit guides, and/or angels, use dreams to communicate **messages of love**.

In dream-visitations, our pets can give us a visual image of themselves in order to show us something that we need to see. It gives them the opportunity to communicate clearly, and sometimes this is done using telepathy. The visual appearance of their physical body allows them to share their new health, their new life, and their new beginnings in the Afterworld.

Not only this, dream-visitations give us another chance to

see our sweet pets again, even if it is only for a short moment in time. They know how much we miss them and how badly we yearn to be with them. If they can, they will certainly try to visit during our sleep state.

Visitation dreams are very easy to identify. One of the truest distinctions is how *real* everything feels. Upon waking, you would swear the experience was as authentic as your conscious state. You might even think, "Wow, that felt so real. It truly felt like he (or she) was right here with me."

The dream-visitation will also be very vivid. So clear in fact, that your memory of the events will not be forgotten. You will remember them for days, months, years... quite possibly your entire life.

The beloved companion who appears to you will almost always be healthy and behave in a very loving manner. The intent of your special one is to share their love with you. They want you to know that their pain has been released, their sadness is gone, or their illness has now been removed.

Robin's cat, Amber, wanted her to know how much he loved her. Through a dream-visitation, he was able to calm her grief.

*Before I was ever a believer, I had experienced a dream after I put my cat, Amber, to sleep. I was devastated and had no idea you grieve the same way about your pets as you do humans.*

*Amber came to me strongly, telling me I didn't need to grieve so hard. He told me he felt much better where he was and that he would see me when it was my time to cross, but that wouldn't be for a long time. The dream, now known as a visit, was so comforting and crystal-clear. I will never forget it as it feels like I dreamt it just yesterday. A very gifted medium explained to me that the message came through to me in English because the universal language for spiritual communication is telepathy. Everything is translated for us so that we can understand spiritual communication. What a precious gift Amber has given me. ~Robin Tait, Toronto, Ontario (Canada).*

**Messages tend to** be very reassuring. Through telepathy, pets can share the same words humans do. You might hear phrases like, "I'm okay. I'm safe. I love you." Or maybe have the sense of hearing, "Please don't be sad. I'll always be with you."

Many report feeling a sense of peace and love upon waking from a visitation dream. Others report feeling very sad, having not realized, or believed, that their pets can and will communicate after their physical death.

Oftentimes, they will also visit other members of your family, or friends, to let them know they are okay. They might even give information that needs to be delivered to you.

These types of visitation dreams are considered, *third-party visits.* This becomes an easy way for your pet to deliver a message directly to you. There might not be words attached to the special delivery, but the presence of the being, the happiness in the bark, the glow of their fur, the smile on their face, the wagging of their tale; these too are very prominent indications of a beautiful connection between you and your pet.

As a side note, normally a *third-party visitation* occurs for those who are in very deep grief, or for those who have been unable to remember their dreams.

Whatever communication is shared will be very clear. They may speak to us by showing us a symbol or by using telepathy. When they use telepathy, you will remember that you heard their voice—yes, on the other side, our pets can and do speak to us. When Sandra experienced her Yorkie in a visit, she knew her baby was okay.

*Lexie was diagnosed with a very aggressive cancer last year. She was thirteen-years-old and there was nothing the vet could do. Their suggestion was to take her home and enjoy every minute with her. For the next two months, I laid on the couch with her nightly on what I called her hospice blanket. I looked into her big brown eyes and asked, "Lexie, when you get to the rainbow bridge, will you please give me a sign so I know you made it?"*

*I told her how wonderful it would be when she got there and she just stared into my eyes and gave me this look as though she knew exactly what I was saying. About a month after she passed, I came across Lyn Ragan's Facebook page (the author of this book) and saw a picture of Lexie standing at the rainbow bridge. I was floored and tears filled my eyes. I knew it was her letting me know she made it safely. However, the best sign of all happened last month. I had a visitation dream.*

*It was very vivid and VERY real. Lexie was there with her curly wild hair. She was beautiful and looked like a new puppy. I cried out to her, "Lexie, is that you?" Then, I woke up very happy and very peaceful. I know without a doubt, Lexie was letting me know she is okay. ~Sandy R., Stuart, Florida.*

**Oftentimes, one might** feel dazed or confused, not able to tell if they were awake or asleep when they saw their deceased pet. Such is the case for Belinda, when her Poodle unquestionably appeared before her.

*When I was thirteen, I fell in love with our little black poodle, Charlotte. She went everywhere with me; to the beach, the park, friends' houses, and she slept with me every night too. One evening, Charlotte ran in front of a car and was hit. I screamed and cried while I tried to give her mouth-to-mouth resuscitation, but I could not save her. She died a few minutes later. I have never cried so hard. I missed her terribly and couldn't bear to sleep without a nightlight on in my room. I can't say if I was awake or if I was asleep, but I sensed her very near. As I glanced around the room, there Charlotte sat. In front of the nightlight. Looking at me.*

*I often wondered if Charlotte came to me that night to say good-bye. It took a long time to heal after her death I loved her so much. ~Belinda O., Victorville, California.*

**Our pets can** give us a visual image of themselves, or a clear picture of an occurrence, in order to show something they want us to know. This happened to Lynn when her sweet companion, Ruby, showed her a particular image.

*My husband and I rescued Ruby, a longhaired Dachshund, when she was two years old. She and I were very close. In May of this year, I dropped her at the vet for a dental cleaning. She was ten and I had no reason to believe there would be a problem. At noon, I received a call stating her surgery went well and I could pick her up at four o'clock. A few hours later, I received another call telling me she couldn't breathe and I needed to take her to a vet specialist. She was diagnosed with aspirated pneumonia and was treated for five days with no results. I had to let her go. I was devastated.*

*When I received Ruby's ashes, I asked her for a sign. Two nights later as I lay in bed, I saw her face come in and out of focus. Then, I saw her sitting on the lap of a woman who was dressed in a white dress. I never saw the woman's face—only Ruby sitting on her lap. I felt relieved, and very comforted, knowing that Ruby was okay. ~Lynn P., Palm Harbor, Florida.*

**The vision Pamela** received when her dog went missing gave her a special kind of hope.

*On Valentine's Day two years ago, my dog, Judah, went missing. He always answered my calls quickly, but this time I knew something was wrong. After a hard twenty-four hour search, we hadn't found him. The next day I walked into my yard next to the woods, where I had already searched, and I saw a vision of him running to me. The image of him was so strong and so clear, I cried with joy and a renewed hope.*

*Two hours later, I felt Judah near. I walked outside to that same spot in the yard where I had felt drawn to earlier, and there he was. Sadly, a drunken neighbor had hit him on one of the dirt roads near our home and left him for dead. Somehow, Judah pulled his body using only his front paws over a great distance and made it home. His pelvis was broken in three places, but he has recovered fully. He runs just as strong today as in the vision I saw that gave me hope. ~Pamela K., Panama City, Florida.*

**Dream-visitations and** Visions overflow with peace and love. Our very special pets, here and on the other side, only want for one thing… to let us know their love is unconditional.

# 9

# Angel Numbers

*Having a soft heart in a cruel world is courage
not weakness. ~Katherine Henson*

N umbers are big in the Afterlife. Really big. Because we
already mark times and remember dates for everything
we do; birth, death, dinner, work, weddings, special occasions,
etc., it's simple for our pets to remind us they are close by
through symbolic signs such as numbers.

Significant numbers can begin to appear everywhere we
look. Especially around the holidays. We might start seeing our
pet's birthday, or the date of their passing, or the *time* they
were born and/or transitioned. We might also notice triple
digits materializing, having never seen them before.

It doesn't matter where we see the numbers either. They
can show up on a clock, a watch, the back of a semi, a mailbox,
an address, a Facebook post, a license plate, a sign, a book, a
magazine, or online while browsing.

Recognizing and interpreting the numbers along our pat
can help us feel more closely connected to our pets and to our
angels. This connection allows our pets to open the door to an
incredible relationship that carries peace, hope, love, and faith.

When we see our number signs, it is important to
acknowledge that our pets are sharing an amazing gift. Number

signs are also known as, *Angel Numbers*; communicated messages where sequences of numbers are seen. Always remember to say, thank you, for their communications and for continuing your relationships beyond the veil.

Years ago, I stumbled upon a site that helped me interpret number signs from my fiancée, Chip. At the time, I had no idea how important the messages were and within weeks, I started following his 123 sign wherever it took me; he died on 1/23/08.

Joanne Walmsley is the creator of a wonderful website that helps interpret number signs from our pets on the other side. She has truly designed a very informative home for all to visit and study. Here is her site's web address:

*sacredscribesangelnumbers.blogspot.com.*

On her home page, Joanne shares this very important message about repeating numbers, *"The main thing about seeing and acknowledging the repeating number sequences is the fact that you are consciously seeing them. At this time, your angels are communicating directly with you. The messages are for you and they are about you and your life. It is up to you to take the time to go within, listen to your intuition and true self, and figure out what the messages are telling you and what they mean to you. Only you know what lies within you."*

**Listening to our** intuition and our inner gut instinct is the spiritual riches that lives in us all. Learning how to listen to it, however, is where many of us have a little difficulty.

Our pets in spirit gift us with a *number sign* and that alone is a blessed treasure. If we so choose, we can go one step further into defining what the number sign represents. Listed below is a very short list from Joanne's site of sequential numbers, or Angel Numbers, and their spiritual meanings.

**111**—Take note of your thoughts. Monitor them carefully and think about what it is you really want for your highest good… not what you don't want.

**1111**—An opportunity is opening up for you and your thoughts are manifesting to form at lightning speed. Think only positive thoughts, using the positive energies of the universe to bring to fruition your deepest desires, hopes, and dreams. (Learn more about this angel number at the end of this chapter.)

**222**—Everything will turn out for the best in the long-term. Be aware that all is being worked out by Spirit for the highest good of everyone involved.

**2222**—Newly planted ideas are beginning to take form and grow into reality for you. Your manifestation will soon be evident, so maintain a positive attitude and continue with your good work. The reaping of rewards is just ahead of you.

**333**—Have faith in humanity. The angels are working with you on all levels. They love, guide, and protect you. Always. If you're feeling perplexed or confused as to your life purpose, call upon the angels to assist. They are waiting for your call.

**3333**—Your angels are near you at this time, reassuring you of their love, support, and companionship. Call upon the angels often. They are aware of your position or situation and know the best way to go about things for the highest good. They will help and guide you through your next life phase; they wait for you to call upon them.

**444**—You have nothing to fear. All is as it should be, and all is well. Things that you have been working on, or with, will be successful. You are being surrounded by angels who love and support you. Their help is close at hand, always.

**4444**—You are surrounded by your angels. They are at your side to reassure you of their presence, love, and help. They encourage you to continue working toward your goals and aspirations as success and achievement are ahead of you. If you need it, help is nearby; all you need to do is ask for angelic assistance and guidance.

**555**—Major life changes are in store for you in a very big way. Angel number 555 tells us that significant transformations are here and you have an opportunity to break out of the chrysalis and uncover the amazing life you truly deserve as a spiritual being. Your true life purpose and path are awaiting you.

**5555**—A message from the universe that your life is about to go through some major changes with new freedoms, and the opportunity to live your inner-truths.

**666**—It's time to focus on your personal spirituality in order to balance and heal any issues in your life. Be open to receiving help, love, and support from both humans and angels, as it is there for the taking. Be receptive in order to receive and accept the help you need.

**6666**—Your angels ask you to balance your thoughts between the spiritual and material aspects. Maintain faith and trust that your needs will always be met. The angels ask you to focus on spirit and service, and to know that your material and emotional needs will automatically be met as a result.

**777**—You have listened to Divine Guidance and are now putting that wisdom to work in your life. It is time to reap the rewards for your hard work and efforts. Well done! Your success is inspiring, helping, and teaching others by positive example. This number is a positive sign and means that you should expect miracles to occur in your life.

**7777**—You are on the right path and doing well. Due to your hard work and positive efforts, you have earned your rewards. Your wishes and desires are manifesting and coming to fruition in your life. This number is an extremely positive sign and means that you should also expect more miracles to occur for you.

**888**—Your life purpose is fully supported by the Universe. A phase in your life is about to end; this is a sign to prepare you and your life accordingly. The Universe is abundant and generous and wishes to reward you. Great financial prosperity is yours, now and in the future.

**8888**—There is a light at the end of the tunnel. In addition, it is a message for you not to procrastinate when making your move or enjoying the fruits of your labor. Make the choices that please you. That is your reward.

**999**—The world needs you to utilize your talents and serve your Divine Life Purpose at this time. Fully embark upon your sacred mission without hesitation or delay. *Now* is the time for you to realize your true light and life purpose, and put them into practice.

**9999**—Live your life in a positive and uplifting manner in order to teach others by example. Keep your light shining brightly.

Here are a couple of popular Angel Numbers recognized by thousands.

**911**—A highly spiritual number, 911 encourages you to

pursue your life purpose and soul mission as a Lightworker. Its vibration is of spiritual enlightenment and awareness, and of reaping karmic rewards for work well done.

The angels are telling you that a new door has opened up for you as a product of your positive thoughts, intentions, and actions. Make the most of this opportunity and walk forward with confidence and surety, knowing that you are fulfilling your karmic destiny.

Your goals are almost complete, and/or you are coming to the end of a phase or cycle in your life. It is an indication that one door is closing and another is opening. The message is to allow the old to be released so that it can be replaced with the new.

**11:11**—Be very aware of your persistent thoughts and ideas as these are manifesting quickly into your reality. Ensure that your beliefs, thoughts, and mind-sets, are positive and optimistic in order to draw the energies of abundance and balance into your life.

Look to new beginnings, opportunities, and projects with a positive and optimistic attitude as these are appearing in your life for very good reason. Your angels want you to achieve and succeed with your desired goals and aspirations, so do not hesitate in taking positive steps to strive forward.

Many people associate the repeating 1111 with a *wake-up call,* a *Code of Activation* and/or an *Awakening Code,* or *Code of Consciousness.* It can also be seen as a key to unlock the subconscious mind, and reminds us that we are spiritual beings having a physical experience, rather than physical beings embarking upon spiritual experiences.

Upon noticing a frequency of 1111's appearing repeatedly,

you may begin to see an increase in synchronicities and miraculous coincidences appearing in your life. At times, when you are about to go through a major spiritual awakening, or an epiphany of some kind, the number 1111 may appear in your physical reality to signal the upcoming change or shift.

When noticing the angel number 1111 appearing, take heed of the thoughts you have right at that moment, as 1111 indicates that your thoughts and beliefs are aligned with your truths. For example, if you held an inspired idea at the time of seeing 1111, it would indicate that it would be a positive and productive idea to take action on.

**Another great book** to have on hand is by Doreen Virtue called, *Angel Numbers 101: The Meaning of 111, 123, 444, and Other Number Sequences.* This book explains how to receive accurate messages from angels and loved ones whenever you see repetitive number sequences.

Numbers, or number sequences, are straightforward signs we can witness and follow. Because they exist in everything we do, and we see them everywhere we go, it's easy to spot them as signs if we learn to tune in.

After Angela's dog, Winston, passed away, she started noticing several different signs. One of which was numbers.

*I activated my iPhone and the time shown was 4:44, so I looked up the angel number and this is what it said, "You have nothing to fear. All is as it should be and all is well. You are being surrounded by angels who love and support you. Their help is close at hand, always." I didn't know whether to cry my eyes out or shout and jump for joy! I'm so happy Winston is now my perfect angel. ~Angela T., Harrogate, North Yorkshire.*

**Becoming aware and** watching for number signs helps direct a path where spirit becomes our guide. Numbers are an easy way for our pets to grab our attention. When Marilyn learned her cat was connecting with her, she was stunned.

*For my seventieth birthday, my son gave me a gift certificate for a medium reading. I didn't believe in such a thing and shoved it in a drawer. With the passing of my cat, Miss Patty, I often wondered what happened to her after she died. Twelve years together and now there was nothing.*

*My friends told me to look for Patty's signs, but I thought that too, was hogwash. And then one afternoon my phone rang. It was "that" medium wanting to talk to me. My son took it upon himself to schedule an appointment because he knew I wouldn't do it. I didn't want to, but I listened.*

*My entire family was dead so if she wasn't the real deal, it wouldn't be too hard to figure out if she was full of you know what, real fast. A few minutes into it, she asked me if I had a female cat named Pat, or Patty, on the other side. My mouth dropped. She then asked me if I saw the numbers, 11:11, on the clock. I did. All the time. She asked if I noticed feathers inside the house or on my bed. I did. I found a few in the kitchen and on my bed—how'd she know that?*

*And then she said, "These are Patty's signs for you. When you see them, she wants you to feel her love hugging you. She may have left the physical world, but she will always be with you in spirit." That was the BEST phone call, ever. ~Marilyn B., Jones Prairie, Texas.*

**Number messages from** your pet are very clear when they deliver them… "If you only knew how much you are loved and adored. I am so proud of you."

# Part Two

## Spirit Phenomena

# 10

# Over-Souling

*Earth was created for ALL life—*
*Not just human life.  ~AD Williams*

O ver-souling is a new term for me. It's one I learned about recently due to a direct experience. What is over-souling? In simple terms, it is something one experiences when a pet in Heaven **directs** the behavior and actions of living pets here on earth.

Over-souling occurs when a living pet has agreed to take certain direction from a deceased animal. The direction could be something as easy as teaching a new puppy the rules of the house. For example, the deceased pet might teach the new arrival that he or she is not allowed to chew on the parent's shoes, or tear up books and magazines, or potty on the carpet. Or the direction could be to have the living pet dance like they did in order to show the family they are still with them, but in a different way. Have you ever noticed your pet doing something that reminded you of your deceased pet? Did you make a comment like, "Hey, that's exactly what Roscoe used to do." The characteristics are eerily familiar, and from your pet in spirit, it is considered a **direct visitation** called, *over-souling*.

Many people believe that souls enter into certain contractual agreements before entering the physical vessel to live out life here on earth. Over-souling would be one of those agreements. According to Brent Atwater, an animal medium who sees and talks with pets in spirit, the process of a deceased pet over-souling a living one, is intermittent. Meaning that the actions or the behaviors we notice in our animals that remind us of our deceased pet's characteristics, are short-lived lasting minutes, hours, days, and sometimes even months. But never for the life of our living pet.

Author of, *Animal Reincarnation: Everything You Always Wanted To Know,* Brent Atwater has countless videos and articles sharing a wealth of information about animal communications. In one particular article, she stated that over-soul agreements may *seem* like a pet reincarnation when in fact, they are NOT. Reincarnation is a life process for a pet and is not a short-lived visitation like over-souling.

Can over-souling be seen in humans, as well? The answer is, yes. However, we want to keep our focus on pet behavior. The following story is a perfect example of recognizing familiar personality traits. After Becky and her family took in a second rescue dog, she was shocked to see that her new pet had a few of the same traits her deceased one had. Only months after Abigail had passed from cancer, her soul was preparing another dog for a special journey.

*I received an email from one of Abby's first adopters informing me that a dog had been found in a dry creek bed. She stated he was in bad shape and in need of a home. Because his eyes reminded her of Abby's, she instantly thought of me.*

*We welcomed Charlie into our home last year. Amazingly, he has the **same** happy dance Abby had. Also, he makes some of the <u>same</u> gestures as she did. He can never replace her, but I truly believe Abby sent him to us. Sadly, Charlie has recently* been diagnosed with lymphoma and has a tumor on his heart. We are on another cancer journey, but we know Abby will be the first one to greet Charlie when he crosses the Rainbow Bridge. ~Becky N., Brooklyn Park, Minnesota

**When Sunny and** her friends went to the beach one afternoon, they never in their wildest dreams thought they would experience not one, not two, but three amazing over-soul visitations.

*When my two girlfriends and I arrived on the beach, we all noticed a Labrador dog and its owner playing with a ball. Dogs are allowed on this part of the beach, but rarely had we see them in the past.*

*All of a sudden, the dog raced out of the water and ran up to my friend, Gina. His owner called to him many times, but the lab ignored him. Instead, the dog walked up to Gina, gave her the ball, sat down beside her, and then looked into her eyes. Because Gina had recently lost her own Labrador, she was feeling sad and missing her fur-kid terribly. After the lab left, Gina said she felt like it was **her** dog coming to say hello.*

*After we settled down and got comfortable, we saw another Labrador running along the beach. Much to our surprise, this dog left its owner too and bounded toward Gina. Once the lab reached her, it stood beside her and pressed its face into Gina's leg, staring up into her eyes. It was a remarkable experience. Here's the kicker, though...*

*Later that day, it happened again. A third Labrador appeared on the beach and headed for my friend. Gina was so happy with so many reminders, but also taken aback. She felt the love from her deceased lab and knew it was coming from*

*the three other labs that day. She knew her dog was telling her she was loved and missed, too. We had not seen a Labrador on that beach before this day, or even since. ~Sunny W., North Port, Florida.*

**After laying Dusty** to rest, I thought about her constantly. I received little hints and clues of her spirit being near, but it wasn't anything that made me say, "Aha! That's her." At least not until this happened...

*I was doing laundry one afternoon and not really paying attention to anything else. As I walked through the sitting room, I noticed Scooby (my lab) sitting tall, staring at me. He started to wag his tail wildly, which told me he was up to no good or he had been a bad boy.*

*Then, Scooby did something he had never done before and suddenly, I felt like I was watching a completely different dog. As his head moved slowly from side-to-side, he began to growl a sentence. Of course, it wouldn't be a sentence I could understand in human terms, but it was so crystal clear that I understood every single last vibration.*

*For one, Scooby never growls. Ever. And for two, Dusty growled frequently. It was how she communicated and in her world, Dusty loved to talk. I stopped dead in my tracks and stared into Scooby's eyes. He didn't move and neither did I. Then, the words just crawled across my lips... "Dusty, is that you?" ~Lyn Ragan, Atlanta, Georgia.*

**When we receive** signs from pets in spirit via any type of communication, their messages are incredibly clear... "With all my love, I adore you."

# 11

# Angel Orbs

*Happiness is the richest thing we will ever own. ~Donald Duck*

Have you ever wondered if there's more to life than what meets the eye? If you have, then you might consider a little research project by looking into what is known as, *Angel Orbs*. These orbs are also called, Spirit Orbs.

What is an Angel Orb?

Chances are you've probably seen one before. They are a new phenomenon that have been captured by thousands with a digital camera.

Most orbs show up in photographs as solid or translucent round globes. Some have been captured in the shape of hearts and/or diamonds. Mostly white in color, several spheres have been seen in a multitude of shapes, and sizes. Some will look solid while others appear textured. And some will be in color where others are white.

When an orb appears before us, it may be to simply encourage us or tell us that we are loved. Or it might be to inspire us to have faith when life becomes a bit challenging.

When our angels show up in the form of an orb, it is a simple way for them to share their blessings to those who see them and acknowledge them.

What do the colors of orbs symbolize?

Sometimes the colors can indicate the type of energy present within the orb. The meaning behind the colors usually corresponds to the energy the angel orb is delivering to you, the recipient.

Below is a color list depicting the messages from our pets in spirit:

- **White** – white angel orbs appear more often than colored orbs and that makes sense because guardian angels travel in them. They are also more often present with people, and more visible, than any other type of angel orb. (Guardian angels can be our pets, loved ones, or spirit guides.)
- **Green** – this angel orb is sending you healing energies in the form of divine love.
- **Blue** – this angel orb delivers power, protection, faith, courage, and great strength.
- **Yellow** – the presence of this angel is asking you to remember and embrace your companions in spirit. Giving you its supreme gift, this angel is asking you to embrace love.
- **Pink** – this angel orb is sharing with you the powerful energy of love and the energy of peace. Feel the love. Feel the peace.
- **Red** – this angel orb is offering you its service of wisdom. If you are asking for an answer to a question, you will receive its powerful gift through intellect and deep love.
- **Purple** – this angel orb shares the magic of transformation and asks you to believe, to trust, and to receive love from spirit.

- **Orange** – this angel orb is all about forgiveness. If you are gifted with the presence of this divine colored orb, you are being asked to forgive. You might need to forgive yourself, a perpetrator, a family member, or a friend.

- **Silver** – this angel orb is sharing a beautiful spiritual message with you. Are you asking for proof of ever-lasting life? Are you asking if your pet or angels are near? Your answer is being shown to you.

- **Gold** – this angel orb gifts you with the presence of unconditional love. There is no greater love than that of spirit.

- **Brown** – this angel orb represents the earth plane; to be grounded. Are you spending too much time in the heavens? Eat a hamburger or walk on the grass barefoot—it's time to ground yourself back to earth.

- **Black** – this angel orb is the courier of magic and mystery. Believe in the unseen, for this is where the magic of life was created.

Orbs have been accepted, certainly within the psychic community, as real evidence of spirit presence. They represent the essence, or soul, of a departed pet When a spirit orb, or angel orb, becomes visible in a photograph near a pet, a single person or a group of people, it is a validation of being blessed with the energy and protection of our pets in spirit and our angels.

If you have a camera with a flash, you can ask your beloved pet out loud or silently within, to be in your pictures. They especially love to show up in photos during a celebration like a birthday party, holiday dinners, concerts, etc.

Once you download your photographs, look for the orb(s). Don't be surprised if you see an unknown face, an animal, or a smile within the orb. You might even see your own pet inside of one. Yes, it has happened for others many, many, times.

Several people have reported that when they need guidance or reassurance from their special ones, they have received validation of their presence in pictures. We are indeed, never alone. There are times where we might be lucky enough to catch the sight of an orb with our very eyes. This is exactly what happened to Diane.

*After my cat, Amber, passed away, I kept seeing a bright orb in my bedroom. Every night after I got into bed, it would enter my room from the hall and hover directly over me. There were times I could see numbers inside the orb, but mostly, it was bright and very beautiful. I knew it was Amber letting me know she was still with me. I don't see her as often since I have another kitty. Sometimes though, I do see my new cat look down that same hall, and stare. ~Diane B., Macedon, New York.*

**Orb activity can** bring great comfort and physical validation that our pets in their energy form, are always around us. The last thing Donna would consider herself is lucky, but when she started noticing something unusual happening, that is exactly what we think. She is one of the very few who can actually see her angel orb.

*Two years ago, my little curly handsome, white Bichon Frise was diagnosed with cancer. His name was Hank and he weighed all of twelve pounds. Sadly, because the cancer was so bad, I had to help him go to sleep. Days later, I started seeing* a little white substance floating around my ankles. My other small dog was off sleeping, so I knew instantly this was Hank following me around again. Just like he always did when he was alive; follow me. ~Donna J., Indianapolis, Indiana.

**To see an orb** with the naked eye is quite extraordinary. When I helped my rescue dog cross to the other side, I felt blessed to witness her spirit orb only minutes later.

In the summer of 2014, I adopted two senior dogs from a kill shelter in California. One was a thirteen year old female pit mix, Dusty, and the other was an eighteen year old Chihuahua mix named Scooter. Their story was a sad one and I couldn't help but be moved. I already had two other dogs and figured two more fur-kids would only enhance our lives.

Disappointingly, Dusty did not like my youngest. She was very aggressive and attacked each boy at different points in time. Luckily, I had a plan B—keep them separated until she was more comfortable and reintroduce them at a later time. The plan was moving along and everyone was okay with limited mommy time. It wasn't long before I fell head over heels in love with Dusty. She was almost deaf and her eyesight was horrible. However, her spunk for life and her loving soul melted my heart. As each day passed, a little more of her amazing personality shined through. She loved playing with tennis balls. She enjoyed running at top speed, and she absolutely loved talking through her unusual style of growls. These two new kids had more manners than my other two ever dreamed of having.

Winter was fast approaching and I knew it was time to get everyone in one room playing nicely. I hired a dog trainer and *we worked with Dusty and the boys for hours at a time. She was making amazing progress.*

*November came and from out of nowhere, Dusty stopped eating. After the second day, we headed to the vet's office and soon learned she had a tumor. She had cancer and her time was very limited. I broke down into tears and cried for her. This beautiful dog couldn't catch a break. Her mother passed away and the only family she ever knew took her to a kill shelter with no regard for her life. Now, she had cancer.*

*On November 11, I baked muffins for Dusty's transition. I knew she would be scared once the stranger arrived to give her a shot. I was hoping a few treats would help to ease her fear. I'll never forget that day. How she laid across my lap as I wiped the tears from her eyes. I didn't want her to go.*

*Once Dusty was taken to be cremated, I walked outside with Scooter and just cried. Then, I caught something moving around his body. As I watched Scooter jump from side-to-side, I noticed a little white, translucent, orb-like thing dance all around him. Scooter didn't seem to enjoy it, but I absolutely loved how it nipped at him, flew around his head and then nipped again at his tail, his butt, and his ears. It was a true honor not only to have Dusty steal my heart, but also to witness her in spirit form, playing with her brother. ~Lyn Ragan, Atlanta, Georgia.*

**If we ever** feel the need to prove it to ourselves, we can take a walk outside in the evening, especially during a full moon, and take pictures with our flash. Ask your pet to be there with you and then feel the joy when they appear.

On the other side… LOVE is *everything*.

# 12

# Perfect Timing

*The wind of Heaven is that which blows between*
*a horse's ears. ~Author Unknown*

Sensing Spirit and the timing of events go hand-in-hand. As does the timing of Afterlife communications. Synchronicity plays a big role when experiencing two or more events while they appear closely together.

Beloved pets can choreograph the most organic of messages. This phenomenon is often referred to as connecting with spirit and stepping into the universal flow. Much like what Marti experienced when she felt the closeness of her horse.

*Lady was my baby. She was a beautiful Belgian Draft horse and we were extremely close. She would follow me everywhere I went, much like a dog would, and place her head over my shoulder as we walked. When she passed, I was heartbroken and missed her terribly.*

*One afternoon after feeding our other horses, I was walking through the barn by myself. All of a sudden, I felt the weight of a horse's nose lean across my shoulder and breathe hard against my face. My first thought was that I had left one of the stalls open and a horse had gotten out. When I turned around quickly, there was no horse in sight.*

*As a practicing medium, I instantly knew this was Lady. She wanted me to know she was still here with me, just in a different way. I was blessed with a very beautiful gift—Lady's love. ~Marti T., Reno, Nevada.*

**When Lynda encountered** such a spiritual connection, she had no idea her face-to-face meeting could be so angelic.

*Years ago, I had a Lilac Point Siamese cat named Chris. Chris was very lovable and took every opportunity to sit on my lap. She won my heart as she would crawl up my chest, put one paw around my neck, her head under my chin, and then gently sigh. I was heartbroken when she died in the early eighties.*

*In 2010, my husband was diagnosed with terminal cancer. During the weeks before his passing, something beautiful happened. I was sitting on the deck talking with his daughter when all of a sudden she said, "Look, here comes a kitty." When I turned, I saw an identical Siamese cat walking down the common area of our townhouse community.*

*It strolled right to my deck, up the steps, and over to me. After it sat down and looked at me, the cat then jumped up onto my lap and crawled up my chest. Putting one paw around my neck, it slowly nestled its head underneath my chin. I was stunned.*

*A few minutes later, I saw my husband walking about, so I took the cat inside to show him. As we approached Craig, the cat reached out one paw to him. After I returned to the deck, the cat left, never to be seen again. It wasn't until after my husband's passing and on the heels of the signs I received from him, that I realized the significance of that cat.*

*I went up and down our street to see if anyone owned the cat, but no one did. Nor had they seen one like it. That cat was exactly like my Chris; both in color and in behavior. There could be no denying the fact it was the spirit of my Siamese cat. Chris came that day to comfort not only me, but also a man she never knew. ~Lynda M., Hamilton, Canada.*

**Sensing spirit happens** when we listen to the soft voices. They are life's little way of reminding us to pay attention, to follow the signs, and to watch the path in front of us as it unfolds before our eyes.

The timing of signs are very real and can be an amazing message from our pets. When Ethel volunteered to babysit her daughter's fur-kids, the last thing she expected was to encounter Spirit.

*My daughter had to work out of town one weekend and asked me to stay at her house to take of her dogs. She lost her husband recently and grief had all but stolen her life. The least I could do was take care of her fur-kids.*

*The day was like any other—walk in and get trampled by the big Great Danes. I could see why my daughter loved these giant dogs though. They were such big lovers and enjoyed giving slobbery kisses.*

*At chow time, Jake, the oldest, started barking and running around like crazy. I stopped what I was doing to go inspect. When I walked around the corner, I was nearly attacked. Jake was chasing something around the room and Scarlet, the youngest, soon joined in. It was complete mayhem and to be honest, the whole scene scared me. They were chasing and barking at something that I could not see.*

*I backed up and stood inside the kitchen waiting for them to stop. Out of nowhere, they charged across the floor and that's when I saw it-- a large white and baby blue mist hanging behind Jake's tail. I gasped.*

*After twenty minutes of non-stop running, things calmed down. I called my daughter and cried, informing her that the house was haunted and she needed to move out NOW. She just laughed at me and then told me that it was her husband, Harry. She said he was always playing with the dogs and that's how she knew when he was right there with her. I can't believe I saw it with my own eyes.*

*My beautiful daughter and her amazing husband; cracking the code for love. ~Ethel B., Hilton Head, South Carolina.*

**When we experience** such perfect timing, we are in fact connecting with spirit and stepping into the universal flow of life, all at the same time. Days after Laura's little Pomeranian passed away, surprise was an understatement when her daughter witnessed the spirit of their little dog.

*My Pomeranian, Nola, was killed by a large stray Pit mix. My children were on vacation at the time and I wasn't about to tell them what happened over the phone. Nola was a family member and I knew the kids would be heartbroken. The evening they came home, I broke the news to them, but I omitted the grave details surrounding Nola's death. I simply explained that she needed surgery and did not survive. My eight-year-old daughter cried her eyes out.*

*Then, moments later, she walked over to me and said, "Mommy, Nola just ran through the living room with a large brown dog chasing her. She showed me what happened. The dog attacked her!" I sat there, stunned. There was no way my daughter could have known the details. No way possible. Nola was without a doubt, right there with us. ~Laura P., Poplarville, Mississippi.*

**Sensing your pet** in spirit can be a magical exploration. When we listen to the soft voices and witness the signs from our pets, divine love cradles our hearts.

# 13

# Family Pets

*If there are no dogs in Heaven, then when I die I*
*want to go where they went. ~Will Rogers*

amily pets are a big blessing in disguise. Like children,
the animal kingdom can see spirit. They not only see
them, they can smell them, hear them, and can follow them as
well.

Is there proof that our pets can see spirit? Hard evidence is
very elusive, however, if you have had the extreme pleasure of
watching your pet stand in a corner barking at something that
**you** can't see, then there's a really good chance your pet sees
spirit.

Our pets have a sixth sense like no other. Not only do they
have a keen sense of hearing, they have an exceptional sense of
smell, too. Their senses are stronger and very different from
ours. Their ability to detect movement is heightened more than
ours and their sense of smell is ten thousand times more
sensitive than that of humans. At four times the distance than
someone with normal hearing capabilities, our pets can hear the
higher frequencies of spirit.

Because they can't vocalize and offer their own
explanations of what they see, hear, or smell, there is no way to
know exactly what is going on in those precious moments of
connectivity.

Our pets can be the best detection of spirit for us. When they follow something we can't see, or if they bark, hiss, or their fur raises up on their back, neck, and tails, this is a telltale sign that their connection with spirit is very strong. After Janet lost her dad and sister, her precious dog would let her know when they were near.

*There were many times when I sat on the couch, crying my eyes out, that my dog, Cooper, would start barking. I watched him as he stared up at nothing. At those exact moments, I felt the air change. I could smell my dad and sister's scents, or I felt their presence in the room. But Cooper was the one who always noticed them first. He became my Seeing Eye dog. ~Janet M., Lafayette, Indiana.*

**According to a** recent survey, over forty percent of pet owners believe their pets have a sixth sense. We've come a long way in our beliefs over the years. With science finding it difficult to explain the superior senses of our animals, who's to say pets can't perceive our spirit family.

After Lynn's husband died unexpectedly in November 2014, she noticed one of her dogs acting strangely a few days later.

*In the early morning following my husband's passing, I noticed odd behavior from Ginger, our red shorthaired Dachshund. She awakened and immediately began to whine and cry at something above her, in our bed. Her head was bobbing up and down as if someone was patting her. It was a cry of grief and nothing I had ever heard from her before. I asked her, "Is he here?", but of course, she couldn't answer me. Everything in her behavior indicated she recognized* *someone she knew and adoringly loved-- her dad. Ginger loved to sit with him in his reclining chair and after **that** day, she never jumped on it again. ~Lynn P., Palm Harbor, Florida.*

**Is there proof** that our pets can see spirit? If you were to ask me that question, I would tell you they most certainly can.

*I was heartbroken when Charlie, my fifteen-year-old Chihuahua, passed in 2007. As much as I grieved for him, I had no idea how badly his little mate would be missing him too; getting her to eat was downright difficult. Angel was thirteen then and Charlie was all she had ever known. She came into my life when she was seven weeks old so the two of them grew up together.*

*The week after his passing, I was walking through the living room when I saw Angel sitting at the entrance to the kitchen. I stopped in my tracks to watch her. Any other time, she would sense me near and come running, but she didn't notice me this time. Instead, she stared up at one spot at the corner of the ceiling.*

*I looked up where her eyes were glued, but I saw nothing there. Several minutes went by and Angel just sat there with her eyes piercing a hole in that wall corner. I finally walked closer to her, asking her what she was staring at and surprisingly, she didn't flinch when I spoke to her. So I leaned down beside her, in the same way she was, and tried to see what she was seeing. There was nothing there. Nothing that I could see, that is.*

*Until I touched her, she didn't move. I don't know if it was Charlie she was listening to or if it was another angelic being. My guess is that it was Charlie. Maybe he was telling her he was okay and letting her know she would be okay too. The reason I say that is, after that evening she started to eat again.*

*Angel continued to grieve, badly at times, but with a lot of love and attention, she slowly came back to me. Can animals see spirit? I believe they can. ~Lyn Ragan, Atlanta, Georgia.*

**Like children, our** earth pets can see spirit, too. If we pay attention and watch their behavior, we can use their senses as a guide to help us notice spirit, too. Like Sunny did when she was alerted to her deceased pet's presence.

*For the first year after our Rottweiler's passing, Baby Girl, my husband and I caught glimpses of her walking around the house. We watched her on several occasions enter the living room and lie down on the floor. We also have two Chihuahuas who would bark at a corner in the room. Baby Girl loved the pool. Many times the two small dogs would go to the side of the pool and yap into it as if they could see her in it. We could then "feel" her turn to look at them with that side-glance of hers that she gave when they tried annoying her. Now when we see them barking at the corner or in the pool, we look at each other and say, "Hello, Baby Girl. We miss you so much." She lived to be twelve-years-old and was such a sweet soul. ~Sunny W., North Port, Florida.*

**Is there proof** that our pets can see spirit? Watch your earth pets to find out.

# Part Three

## Nature Signs From Heaven

# 14

# The Ladybug

*I believe all animals were created*
*by God to help keep man alive. ~ Iwao Fujita*

The ladybug symbolizes love and protection and is a very popular sign by devoted companions in the Afterlife. These little wonders of nature are remarkable Gifts.

It is a widely known fact that the appearance of a ladybug indicates a time of luck. The spiritual protection they offer can be a shielding from our aggravations and irritations. They present us with the opportunity to take heed and ask us not to allow the little things to take over our lives.

It has always been considered good luck to have the ladybug—or ladybird, ladyclock, ladycow, lady fly—shine its presence upon you. Even more so, killing them was considered unlucky. Some traditions say you should make wishes upon the ladybug while resting it in the palm of your hand. As the beetle flies away, the wish is released into the universe to be fulfilled.

This mysterious ladybug carries the golden strand that leads to the center of the universe, into past lives, spiritual enlightenment, death and rebirth, renewal, regeneration, fulfilled wishes, fearlessness, protection, good luck, and protection. That is a tremendous amount of responsibility for such a tiny creature.

Their appearance signals new happiness; often with

material gains. With the ladybug as a sign, we can often look at it as an indication of a renewed well-being occurring soon. They tell us that our higher goals can be easier to achieve in the near future.

*What does the ladybug teach?*

The ladybug instructs us to be unafraid to live our own truth. Their message is clear—protect your truth and know that it is yours to honor. Ladybugs teach us that life is short and to let go of our worries and our fears. They want us to trust in Spirit and enjoy our life

*What message is my pet sending by using the ladybug as a sign?*

Ladybugs symbolize love, protection, and good luck. When the beetles appear in our lives, our pets inform us that we're being protected. Their message is clear… "I am your guardian angel and protector. My love is tightly wrapped around you, keeping you safe." They also tell us we can now work at bringing our dreams into our physical reality.

Most importantly, our dear pets let us know we are loved unconditionally. Lynn's experience is a wonderful instance of divine love. She never imagined such a remarkable gift.

*Ginger, my red shorthaired Dachshund, would have been fourteen. She had some health issues the past couple of years and I noticed her decline. Two weeks ago, she stopped eating and I knew it was her time to go.*

*After I received Ginger's ashes, I asked her for a sign. What I received was unique and very creative. Before my mom passed away, we had agreed that her sign for me and my two daughters would be a ladybug. She is very generous in sending signs when either of us asks for one.*

*My daughter had gone to the mall and as she exited a store, she saw a little girl holding two balloons on a string. One balloon was a ladybug and the other was a dachshund. She texted me immediately and said, "Ginger is with Nana."*

*The bonds with our pets are very strong and their death has only strengthened them. I know we will be reunited someday. ~Lynn P., Palm Harbor, Florida.*

**Love is the** key ingredient for continuing relationships with our pets in the Afterlife. Receiving signs from them can truly help change our perspectives in life. Feeling blessed and loved from the other side is exactly what Missy felt upon recognizing a gift from her pit bull.

*My kids were teenagers with tons of activities and my husband worked all the time. Sandy came into my life at a time of utter chaos. During my hike in the park one morning, a dog strolled out of the woods. She was dirty from head-to-toe and definitely a pit bull.*

*The closer I got the faster her tail wagged. As I trotted by, she took a quick sniff of my hand. I did not stop. There wasn't time for that and there certainly wasn't time for loving on a dog. I reached my car, opened the back door to get my water, and from out of nowhere something flew by. That dirty dog was sitting in the back seat of my car.*

*She changed our lives. We named her Sandy because her fur was the color of sand. She was indeed a pit bull and a beautiful one at that. We fell head over heels in love, especially my husband. Sandy was **his** dog. Wherever he went, she was right there with him. If he was mowing the grass, Sandy was in* *the wagon being towed behind the mower. If he was in the shower, she was sitting at the door waiting for him.*

*Sandy was family. When she got sick one afternoon, I thought our world came crashing in. It did for a while. We lost Sandy that night. After thirteen beautiful and happy years, her little life came to a screeching halt. My heart was broken.*

*Two days after her passing, I was cooking dinner. I opened the refrigerator to get milk and when I closed the door, I saw something move. It was a ladybug scooting across a picture of Sandy. A few minutes later, my husband walked in from the garage and shouted, "Mis, look! A ladybug landed on my chest. I shook it off twice and it keeps coming back." We both said it at the same time, "Sandy?"*

*It wasn't until that evening we knew for certain. While we watched TV, I saw something moving in the distance. It was a ladybug crawling across Sandy's picture on her urn. We both started to cry. We knew then she was communicating with us. The best part though? The picture on her urn was one we took a few years back. It was a close-up of her big smile AND a ladybug attached to her nose. Sandy loves her ladybugs, and we love her signs of love. ~Missy R., Enterprise, Alabama.*

**In the Afterlife,** love is everything. Our spirit families want to communicate with us as much as we want to, with them. Learning a new language is hard, but learning *Spirit Language* is even more difficult. Communicating with our pets can change our lives forever. Just like it did for Lisa. When she heard from her cat, she knew everything was going to be okay.

*Earlier this year I had to help my Tabby cat cross to the other side. His name was Oscar and he was my very best friend. This cat wasn't a normal cat. He taught himself to use the toilet instead of the litter box. He would greet me at the door and if I let him, he would lay in my lap for hours. I was devastated when Oscar died. I wept inconsolably.*

*The next day I was staring blankly out the window, drinking my morning coffee and of course, crying and thinking about Oscar. Within seconds of saying out loud, "I love you, Oscar," a single ladybug crawled across the window. Then, another one appeared. And another. Right then, I knew it was him. The ladybugs were Oscar's way of telling me he was right there with me and he loved me too. ~ Lisa M., Columbia, South Carolina.*

**Learning how to** communicate with our deceased pets is worth every ounce of effort we put into it. It does take a tremendous amount of patience and a great deal of practice. But the rewards can be life changing.

When Kim opened her eyes and saw a much bigger picture forming, she knew her life would change forever.

*A few days after my fourteen-year-old German Shepherd passed away, I sat looking up at the ceiling. In my grief, I found myself often staring vacantly at floors, walls, and ceilings. On this particular morning however, I noticed a single ladybug walking along the blade on the ceiling fan. I didn't think anything of it until the next day.*

*Needing something to eat, I drove down the hill to buy some food. I decided to turn on the radio to drown out my sad thoughts. When I reached for the knob on the stereo, a ladybug landed on my hand. I thought about shooing it off, but in that quick second, it was like a light bulb was lit inside my head. I couldn't help but question if the ladybug was a sign from my, Rocky. I helped the beetle onto my dashboard while I went to get something to eat.*

*Upon my return, I was shocked to find not only one ladybug, but many. There were fourteen in all. The same age as Rocky. Is that a sign? Yes, indeed it is. What a blessing still to have him around me for love and support. ~Kim W., Perry, Florida.*

**On the other** side, *Love* is everything...

# 15

# Red Robins

*Man is not the only animal that seeks freedom
and space. ~Anthony D Williams*

The legend of the robin's red breast goes back to the coming of Jesus Christ. It is said that in Jesus' hour of need, the robin is the one that tried to remove the thorns from his head while on the cross. The bird stood guard over Jesus and allowed only the light to come near. Because of this act of bravery, a splash of blood stained his breast and has since then been worn with great pride by all red breasted robins.

When male robins are engrossed in territorial disputes, they sing loudly to each other. This unique trait supports the creative energy of the robin. Using their voice to become spiritual in nature, the robin reminds us to trust our intuition and sing our own song as we move forward in our lives.

The egg of the robin is powder blue. This is the color that is often used to activate the throat chakra in humans. The throat chakra represents communication and expression, while the egg symbolizes new life. In essence, the robin tells us we can learn to express ourselves in a positive way in all that we do. They tell us there's nothing to fear and as we restore faith in ourselves, we are safe while being led to our new beginning.

The robin encourages us to believe in our own abilities and to trust that the right path for each of us will be revealed in its precise time.

*What does the red robin teach?*

The red robin teaches us that any and all changes can be made with joy and laughter. They show us how to move forward with grace, perseverance, and tenacity. The robin teaches us how to incorporate our new beginnings with faith and trust. Their spiritual message is very beautiful—*it's time to sing your own song for this new beginning in your life.*

*What message is my beloved pet sending by choosing the red robin as a sign?*

The robin is also a traditional herald of spring. When this bird crosses our path, we can expect new growth to occur in a variety of areas of our life. When our pets chooses the robin as their sign of choice, their message is a special one… "Feel my energy and allow me to lift your Spirit. Trust yourself. Trust your soul. And, trust me. You know which direction to go. Just go, and everything will fall right into place."

There is no finer messenger than the red robin. With its constant reminder to trust yourself and trust in spirit, how can you possibly go wrong. When Nicole received a message from her best friend, she did just that—she trusted the messenger.

*After returning home from picking up the ashes of my Dachshund, Jenny, a robin walked right up to me outside the garage. I knew instantly it was a sign from her. With tears in my eyes, I kneeled down and kept still while it hopped all around me. It was an amazing experience and one I'll never forget. ~Nicole B., Belmont, Massachusetts.*

**Trust yourself. Trust** your pet. You are not alone.

# 16

# The Hawk

*No matter how your heart is grieving, If you keep on believing,
the dream that you wish will come true. ~Cinderella*

H awks carry the symbolism that comes with the ability to
fly and reach the skies. They can soar high and reach
the heavens effortlessly. The hawk is a superior messenger and
is linked to bringing communications from the spirit world.

Hawks are the protectors and visionaries of the air. They
hold the key to higher levels of consciousness. One trait all
hawks share is the ability to move between the seen and the
unseen realms with grace, while joining both worlds together.
Hawks have a broad vision, allowing them to see what the
future holds. For the human, this is a metaphor of prophetic
insight.

When I received a powerful hawk message, I knew it was
a sign from my little Angel, my sixteen-year-old Chihuahua.
Within minutes of her passing, a messenger appeared.

*My heart was ripped into shreds when I had to let my
Angel girl go. Leaving the vet's office without her in my arms
was so unnatural and one of the hardest things I have ever had
to do.*

*On my drive home, I could barely see the road. I was
crying my eyes out and begging for a sign from anyone in
Heaven to show me that Angel was okay. I needed to know she*

*had made it safely to the other side. For fifteen agonizing minutes, I got nothing. Zilch. Nada. Then, I made my final turn and when I did, I was floored.*

*Soaring from above, an incredibly large bird was headed toward my truck. Because it looked like it was going to slam into the windshield at any given second, I slowed down. In utter shock, I watched as the mammoth bird flew directly in front of the grill of my truck and then like an angel itself, swiftly glided up and over the top of the hood. I stomped on the brakes and jumped out to see where it had gone, but it was nowhere in sight. Just like that, it disappeared.*

*Then it hit me. The bird was a beautiful hawk. As soon as I got home, I looked up its spiritual meaning and learned that the hawk is considered a prophetic messenger. That's all I needed. My sweet baby girl, Angel, had made it home safely and her sign to me was this amazing bird—the hawk. ~Lyn Ragan, Atlanta, Georgia.*

**Hawks are a** perfect companion to develop our spiritual awareness. They signify joining together with *all that is.* The hawk is a bird of the heavens, arranging the changes necessary to prompt our spiritual growth and our awareness.

*What does the hawk teach?*

The hawk gives us the ability to see meaning in ordinary experiences. Many of the messages the hawk brings us are about freeing ourselves of thoughts and beliefs. Ones that are limiting our ability to soar above our life and gain a greater perspective. The ability to ascend beyond to catch a glimpse of the bigger picture helps us to survive and flourish.

When Jake's Great Dane passed away from cancer, he

thought he had lost him forever.

*Moose was a big mushy dog and had the heart of a king. He was my very best friend and when he got sick, my heart broke for him. I saw the pain he was in and sadly, there was nothing I could do except thank him for enriching my life. In the short ten years we spent together, he had changed me completely.*

*The day after his death, I sat out on my deck alone. This was normally the time that Moose would sit on top of me while we watched the sun go down. The forest butts up against my property so it's not unusual to see an abundance of bird activity. Today however, as I silently wished for Moose to be with me, a large bird appeared out of nowhere. It was one I hadn't seen before and its wingspan stretched for miles—or so it seemed.*

*When it landed on the railing just a few feet from where I sat, my breath was stolen. I wasn't sure if I should run or be very still. I chose the latter. As we stared each other down, I realized what was sitting in front of me was a tremendously large and beautiful red tailed hawk. I sensed no fear from this bird. For five long minutes, we exchanged eye contact and just as it appeared, the bird stretched its wings and flew off into the woods.*

*I was utterly amazed and to be quite honest, in those few minutes of time my grief for Moose was null and void. Then, I remembered something. I had recently read somewhere that the hawk is a phenomenal messenger from spirit.*

*Could it be possible? I wondered. I decided to accept that this magnificent experience was a sign from Moose. I chose to carry the faith that it was indeed possible to exist in a different way after we leave this earth. I am so glad I did. Because now any time I feel weak and heartbroken, a hawk appears. Every time I miss Moose in an extreme way, this wonderful creature crosses my path. I know Moose loved me when he was here in his physical body, but now I know he loves me even more in his spirit one. I am one lucky dad. ~Jake E., Cumberland, Maine.*

**What message does** a pet send by using the hawk as a sign?

With our eyes closed, visions appear. When we cannot see, is when we see the most. When you notice the hawk, be aware that a message is received and needs to be interpreted. This amazing bird holds the key to higher consciousness and the circle of awareness.

When your beloved pet delivers this remarkable bird upon your path, their message is a very brave one… "I'm here. I love you. Please know that your enlightenment is imminent. Take me with you."

**When the hawk** shows up in your life, be sensitive to the messages it may carry and be receptive to your own intuition. Your pet is connecting with you and wants you to know you are divinely loved.

# Red Cardinals

*Know that the same spark of life that is within you is within all of our animal friends… the desire to live is the same within all of us. ~Rai Aren*

T he red cardinal is a symbol of vitality and offers safe passage into the realm of personal power to realize one's own goals and dreams. They help deliver a balance of intuition, perseverance, and incredible strength.

The red cardinal is also a big representation of the Afterlife. Many have reported that a cardinal appears just before or after a death. In addition, reports show that a cardinal frequently visits or shows up in dreams after the loss of a loved one or the loss of a dear pet.

The red cardinal is easy to spot due to the male bird's spectacular color. As one of the most popular bird species, it is often associated with Christmas and the winter season due to its bright and cheerful appearance.

The red color of the cardinal is very symbolic in nature. It stands for hopefulness, reminding us to *keep the faith*, even when our circumstances look bleak and hopeless.

With their dazzling red hue and powerful call, the cardinal stands out in a crowd. In times of sadness and grief, it may be possible for a simple red bird to get our attention when nothing else can. That's exactly what happened when Anne got the shock of her life.

*A few days after Gayle passed away, a cardinal flew into my house. Gayle was my nine-year-old Chocolate Labrador and was a beautiful dog, inside and out. She always had fatty tissues showing up on her body, but one of them turned out to be cancerous. In a few short weeks, it took her life.*

*My son left the door open on his way out, but only for a minute, and the next thing I knew I was staring at a red bird sitting on the back of a chair next to me. I was shocked. I watched him as he looked around, cocked his bright red head a few times, and as quickly as he appeared, he flew back out. It was an amazing gift and one I cherish every day. Anytime I ask Gayle for a sign now, she delivers a red cardinal and in an instant, I feel comforted. ~Anne F., Mt. Pleasant, Michigan.*

**What does the** *red cardinal teach?*

The cardinal's voice is strong and clear and reflects an air of importance. This power-packed bird can teach us how to express our truth, develop confidence, and walk our talk. If we respect its teachings, it will lead us home.

*What message is my pet sending by using the red cardinal as a sign?*

The red cardinal symbolizes importance and faith. There's no surprise this bird is often chosen as a messenger to deliver a meaningful declaration. One that says... *Spirit is with you.*

Using the cardinal as their sign, our pets remind us that passion, warmth, and strength is available to us. Especially while we're under that cover of dark grief.

When our pets deliver a red cardinal as their preferred gift, they share a very beautiful message... "I'm right here with you. When you think of me, please know I am beside you, giving you warmth and strength. I love you."

Our pets in spirit are always trying to let us know they are near. Dixie knows this all too well. She received quite the surprise when her granddaughter delivered a wonderful gift.

*I truly believe Nilla sends me cardinal signs. Nilla was my eleven-year-old Siberian Husky. We were so close and I miss her terribly. She died a few weeks ago after having surgery for a cyst removal.*

*The other day a female cardinal was here with a male and I thought that was odd. We don't usually see females as often as the bright red males. When my five-year-old granddaughter came to visit that afternoon and saw the female too, she shouted, "Grammy, there's your Nilla."*

*Her signs let me know she's still here with me and that brings great comfort. ~ Dixie M., Dayton, Ohio.*

**Asking for a** sign is perfectly fine, too. Like Paige did. After her Basset Hound passed, she sat and talked to him to stay connected to his spirit.

*Charley was a big hound and loved his life. He showed such joy in everything he did or touched. He should have been a cat because his curiosity was much bigger than he was. Sadly, a neighborhood dog jumped our fence and attacked Charley. His wounds were too great and two days after the attack, he passed away. My heart was broken, but I refused to believe he was forever gone. I started talking to his spirit, asking him for a small sign to let me know he was okay.*

*The next day, I was outside in my backyard when I noticed a red cardinal following me about. He was very noisy, much like Charley was. He flitted about and quickly grabbed my attention. I know that bird was a big sign from my little guy. He continues to bring me comfort every day. ~Paige D., Hampton, South Carolina.*

**In this circle** of life, the red cardinal reminds you of the importance of yourself as an individual. You are loved and divinely adored.

# 18

# The Dove

*Lots of people talk to animals… not very many listen though.
That's the problem. ~Benjamin Hoff*

T he voice of the dove is a graceful song that brings us great hope of a new beginning. Their somber coo speaks to our souls and stirs our inner emotions.

The dove is the symbolic link between Mother Earth and air. Their soft calming coos and tame appearance only enhances their reputation as celestial messengers.

They are also a symbol of the soul's release from its earthly duty. They represent peace of the deepest kind, the type of peace, which enables us to renew our thoughts in the silence of our minds. It is in these moments of stillness we can truly appreciate the simple things in life.

The dove's singing appears when the veil between our physical and spiritual world is at its thinnest; first thing in the morning and late in the evening. This shows how they represent a bond between two realms. When Brandi recognized her message, she felt more love and more peace than she could have ever imagined.

*Toto was the love of my life. She was my little wizard from Oz and I loved her so. After ten wonderful years together, she passed away in her sleep. I was devastated. Three days after she died, I looked out my window and saw a bright white dove sitting on the sill staring at me through the glass. I heard a phrase some time ago—"to see a dove is to see your pet from Heaven." Toto was visiting me from Heaven. The peace I felt in that moment was so strong, it lifted the blues from my very soul. ~Brandi M., Lansing, Michigan.*

**The dove is** the bringer of peace. They understand gentleness. Carrying the energy of peace, the dove reminds us to ward off the negativity from our thoughts, our words, and feelings, for goodness surely awaits us. The peace they deliver allows us to receive the gifts they present:

- Emotional healing
- Physical healing
- Mental healing
- Spiritual healing

*What does the dove teach?*

The dove teaches us that regardless of our circumstances, peace is always a breath away. Harmony and serenity is within us and is always available. When the dove flies into our lives, they ask us to go within and release emotional disharmony from the past and the present.

*What message is my pet sending by using the dove as a sign?*

Signs from our pets come from their heart center. If their messenger touches you, then it is a sign. When the dove is sent to cross your path, your loving pet is sharing a very beautiful message… "Mourn what has passed, but awaken to the promise of the future. New waters and new life are still possible. I'm here with you."

**Let me show you the way.**

# 19

# Hummingbirds

*The more I appreciate the blessings I have, the more blessings I find.  ~Alan H. Cohen*

T he only creature to stop dead in its tracks while traveling at top speed, this tiny bird adapts easily to any situation. They bring *love* like no other messenger can, and their perfect presence delivers joy to those who observe it.

These tiny wonders of mystery are very symbolic in nature. They represent the absolute highest energy of joy. Deemed "The Messenger," the hummingbird stands for *stopper of time* as well as *healing*.

A little known fact about this magnificent bird is the fluttering of its wings. Moving in the shape of an infinity sign, the hummingbird solidifies their great connection to eternity, continuity, and infinity. They are also a symbol of resurrection. On cold nights, their bodies hibernate, seeming to die. At the break of sunrise, they come back to life.

*What can the hummingbird teach?*

Able to fly backwards, they educate and inform us that it's okay to look back into our past and visit those special memories of our deceased pets. We also discover that regret and feelings of guilt are unwarranted.

When the hummingbird hovers over flowers feeding on

sweet nectar, they show us we should savor every moment and appreciate the people we truly love. They remind us to seek out the good in life and the beauty in each day.

Hummingbirds open our hearts. From the pain that caused us to close ourselves off, they offer their extraordinary love until we are free to explore again. Jill's experience is a great example of finding love in a very small package. After her pot-bellied pig passed away, she never dreamed of feeling such joy from a hummingbird.

*After Hank died, a friend told me to look for signs of his continued existence. One of the few lucky people on this planet, my experience with death has been very limited. Because of that, any acknowledgement of an afterlife was non-existent. I really did want to believe it was possible, to speak with the dead, but until I saw it with my own eyes I knew I wouldn't believe it.*

*However, I did start a journey into self-discovery. I searched the internet for information, I read blog after blog, I joined a few groups on Facebook, and I purchased several books on animal communications and afterlife signs.*

*A few weeks after Hank's passing, I sat on the front steps thinking about him and wondering if he was okay in Heaven. From out of nowhere, I heard a gentle buzzing sound whisk around my head, but when I looked, I saw nothing there. It happened again and as soon as I lifted my head, a magnificent little hummingbird appeared in front of my eyes.*

*As I watched it jerk side-to-side, it seemed to stare right at me. I slowly extended my hand and much to my surprise, the weightless creature landed on my finger. This had never happened to me before and after recently reading about the hummingbird being a messenger from spirit, I knew without a doubt my pot-bellied pig, Hank, was behind this magical moment. Since that day, every time I visit the front steps, hummingbirds are by my side within minutes-- my sure fire sign of being close to Hank's spirit. ~Monica D., Bruce, Mississippi.*

**What does the** *hummingbird message mean?*

When our loyal companions send us this incredible sign, they are in essence transporting their unconditional love, devotion, and phenomenal beauty. When we see the hummingbird, time stops while we gaze at its splendor and its quickness. We are touched, loved, and have been given the greatest of luck.

The idea of time standing still, is often relative to a couple in the first months of falling in love. The hummingbird is remarkably brave and not afraid of predators. This detail symbolizes *love* conquering anything... even death.

The greatest gift from the hummingbird is its message: *The sweetest nectar of life lives within.* When our pets deliver this sweet bird as their sign of choice, their message is very special... "Our love conquers anything; even death. I'm here, with you."

*How do I know if the hummingbird is a sign?*

The easiest thing we can do is to question how we're feeling when we cross paths with this creature. Do you feel joy? Are you experiencing love? Do you now wonder if the small beauty can be a message from your deceased pet? Check yourself first, and then analyze the message you are receiving.

There are times when a message won't be seen until the

event itself has calmed a bit. Tina's first experience with a hummingbird is a perfect example of such an occasion.

*My husband purchased a cruise long before our dog, Shelby, died. Though it was three months since her passing, I felt terribly guilty for leaving her behind. I know it sounds silly, but I missed her beyond descriptive words.*

*Ten years ago, I was with a friend who volunteered to walk and exercise the dogs at a local shelter. Shaking hard behind thick bars that surrounded her in a concrete jail cell, then four-year-old Shelby was very sad and oh so scared. And no wonder too. It was loud, raining, and freezing cold. Later I would learn that the only parents she had ever known dumped her off hours earlier. The reason? Because they were sick and tired of cleaning up after her. My stomach flip-flopped as I couldn't imagine the sudden shock she was feeling. I begged to become her new mommy and three days later, she came home to stay. Shelby is the best thing that has ever happened in my life. The connection between the two of us was that of mother and child. She wasn't just a dog. Shelby was half-human and utterly filled with untainted love.*

*My husband and I went on that cruise. In the middle of the ocean one afternoon, we stood on the deck together staring at the beauty before us. We were talking about Shelby when from out of nowhere, almost like magic, a hummingbird appeared in front of us. Yes, a hummingbird. It hovered for about two minutes before it flew away. My husband shouted, "Did that just happen?" Yes indeed, it did. Shelby was on the cruise, too.*
*~Tina C., Jupiter, Florida.*

**Hummingbirds deliver *love* like no other messenger can.**

# 20

# Feathers

*If we could read the minds of animals, we would find only truths. ~Anthony Douglas Williams*

S ymbolizing spiritual evolution to the higher planes, feathers often deliver peace, joy, and the feeling of lightness. They are looked at as a direct link to the realms of the Afterlife.

Above all, feathers come to us as gifts. When we find them along our path, it can mean that we are on a spiritual journey, whether we accept it or not. They can also be an emblem of encouragement as we travel along our voyage.

When angels are near, feathers appear. It's really quite true. It takes a special moment, a sacred space, to see the beauty of a divine feather.

The cool thing about finding feathers is that angels and our pets in spirit place them in our path at just the right time to offer love, validation, and comfort. When we find them, it may be right at the time when we're thinking about making a change, remembering a special memory of a loyal pet, or worrying about someone or something. Feathers can also be a simple reminder that our pets are near and they want us to know it.

A perfect example of this type of reminder happened to Angela after her dog, Winston, passed. Not just once, but many times.

*Seventeen weeks ago, I lost the love of my life, my Rhodesian Ridgeback named, Winston. Since his passing, I see white feathers everywhere I go. I have two other dogs and every walk we go on, there is a white feather as part of our journey... and sometimes at the end of it, too.*

*Just the other day, my younger dog was walked and was put out on the deck to dry off. Over our deck is a glass canopy to provide shelter. Even though the sides are open, the birds will not fly into it because it looks like a closed structure. When I went to let Otis, my younger dog, into the house, I stopped dead in my tracks. Lying on the deck was a white feather. This wasn't an ordinary-looking feather. This was a special and very fluffy kind of feather.*

*I know Winston's energy is with me always. His signs give me a sense of peace and great comfort. ~Angela T., Harrogate, North Yorkshire.*

**Feathers are left** along our path as messages. We might find them on the grass when we go for a walk, or discover them sitting next to our car, or see one by the front door, and always when we can't miss seeing them. Each time we pick one up, it is a reminder we are at the right place at the right time.

When Betty and her husband lost their loving friend, they were surprised at the appearance of feathers when they grieving the hardest.

*When I have a lot on my mind, I talk to my mother in Heaven, in my mind. Later, I always find a feather in the house from her. This past February, I had to do one of the hardest things I've ever done in my life. I had to take my dog, Pee Wee, whom I loved as much as my child, to the vet to be put to sleep.*

*I was crying my heart out and just as I put my Pee Wee in the car, a feather dropped right in front of me. I knew it was a perfect sign from above that my baby boy was going to be okay, but it didn't make the pain of his passing less hurtful.*

*A few months later, I had to put my other dog, Wrangler, to sleep too. The pain was too much to bear. My husband was especially close to Wrangler. Every day for thirteen years, he took his little buddy for a doughnut. The day after Wrangler's passing, my husband leaned against his truck and sobbed uncontrollably. I tried to console him, telling him that his little buddy would always be with him.*

*Just as I said those few words, I looked down. Sitting right there on the truck door was a beautiful white feather. A perfect reminder that we're never alone. I save all of my feathers now, and frame them. The continued love from our pets is amazing.*
*~BettyJane H., Groshen, New Jersey.*

**Feathers also remind** us that we walk in a world overflowing with meaning. Sometimes feathers can become a symbol of reassurance by appearing to us when we are going through a different phase in our life. They tell us we are loved and watched over. They remind us that we are still a part of the whole. The feather creates the opportunity to awaken our insights. They can also represent a fresh start in a spiritual sense, as well as truth, love, lightness, and flight.

The next time we find a feather, we can look at it as a reminder that our dear pets and our angels are with us always.

*What can a feather teach us?*

Birds hold knowledge of speaking with all animals. All

feathers relate to Spirit and its innate connection with the Divine. *Initiators of air*, feathers teach us to open ourselves to the realms beyond physical time and space.

*What message is my pet sending by using a feather as a sign?*

Whatever the circumstance, our pets have a perfect way of reminding us they are with us, bringing comfort, hope, and love. When they use the feather as a sign, they share a very special message… "I'm here with you, watching over you. Use my inspiration to soar into new heights."

As an additional benefit, we can also use the symbols of color to translate our pet's message when they share a feather with us:

- **White**: Your angel reminds you they are here.
- **Yellow**: Congratulations, you are on the right path.
- **Blue**: You are being called to work with Spirit. Your psychic abilities are unfolding. Trust your intuition.
- **Pink**: Love is in the air. Something very special is on the horizon.
- **Gray**: Your life has been hectic. Peace is upon you now.
- **Black** and **White**: Change is coming. Look for it.
- **Black**: Your pet in spirit is protecting all of your energy at this time while you awaken. You are truly loved.

**Your devoted companion** is always with you and is always trying to communicate with you. Know that when a feather appears, your pet is there.

# 21

# Butterflies

*Our perfect companions never have fewer than four feet.*
*~Author unknown*

S ymbolizing celebration, transitions, new beginnings, time, and most importantly, rebirth after death, the butterfly is the courier of joy, peace, and love.

When we think of transformation, the image that comes to mind is usually that of the butterfly. Floating on top of a breeze, this beautiful little creature transports a wisp of joy directly into the heart of its admirer.

What we often fail to think of is its amazing journey from caterpillar to butterfly. Their development process is called *metamorphosis*; a Greek word meaning transformation or change in shape.

Once their physical body has altered, the butterfly must then find its way out of its old form. Digging through the silky shell it created as the caterpillar, it escapes the cocoon and ventures out into a new world.

The butterfly exists in four distinct forms (egg, larva, pupa, and adult), and many consider that we do, as well. For example, a fertilized egg is placed inside our mother's womb and from birth, we are like the caterpillar whose only objective is to eat, gestate, and crawl through life.

Upon our death, we are similar to the sleeping pupa in its

cocoon state, but then our consciousness emerges from the human body and our *soul* is reborn. When we observe the manifestation of the butterfly, we can see how closely tied to their symbolic nature we really are.

These *wonders of nature* are remarkable symbols.

**Butterflies are messengers of the moment.** This is why so many people recognize them as signs from the afterworld. They embody the process of transformation and are a very popular sign by our pets in the Afterlife. When Julie received a validation from her golden retriever, the joy she felt was immeasurable.

*After Blondie died, I experienced a type of grief I had never felt before. My siblings, my mother, my grandparents were all gone and I grieved for each of them. I know that dark sadness that steals your heart. When my sister was murdered, my sorrow was even darker than it had been over all the others. However, when Blondie, my golden retriever of fourteen years, died, it felt like I had lost my child. I could not stop crying.*

*A week after her passing, I was taking out the garbage. As I walked back from the end of my driveway, I noticed a white butterfly following me. Not only did it follow me, it circled around my head more times than I could count. I did wonder if it was Blondie, but I let that thought subside once inside the house. An hour later, I went to the kitchen to fetch a drink. When I entered the doorway, I stood in disbelief.*

*Sitting on the counter, **right next to** Blondie's medicine, was THAT white butterfly staring directly at me. I knew instantly it was Blondie giving me a sign. Like her, solid white in color, was this amazing sign—the messenger of life. I now* *believe in signs. ~Beverly W., Constantine, Kentucky.*

**How do I** *know if it's a sign?*

Oftentimes, butterflies appear when we least expect them. If you are outside gardening, sitting on your patio, or taking a walk, and one happens to flutter in front of you or even land near or on you, do not dismiss it. Since their appearance has garnered your attention, they show themselves for a very good reason.

*What can the butterfly teach us?*

The butterfly is the power of air and has the ability to float on the tip of a breeze. They appear to dance among the flowers as they remind us not to take life so seriously. They awaken a sense of joy as they tell us to lighten up and look for change.

Representing the never-ending cycle of life, the butterfly teaches us that growth and change isn't as traumatic as we've been led to believe. Change can occur gently, and as joyfully, as we wish it to.

These wonders of nature are indeed remarkable symbols. The next time you see a butterfly appear out of nowhere, try to take time to sit within the moment. Ask yourself, "Could this be a message from my pet?" By asking this simple question, we are allowing ourselves to be open to a new way of talking with spirit.

As we move forward in our spiritual growth, the colors of the butterfly can deliver a personal message as well. It's a good idea to get into the habit of documenting a sign when it appears. Each one may have a divine meaning that can help answer questions about everyday life, or quite possibly the path in which you are traveling. You can use a journal to jot your messages or simply record a memo on your phone.

*What do the colors symbolize?*

- **White**: You are divinely connected with your pet in spirit. Look at the bigger picture that's being painted for you.
- **Purple**: Signs are all around you. Trust your gut; you know the truth.
- **Blue**: It's okay to talk to your angel in spirit. Communication is key to continuing this relationship-- talk.
- **Green**: This love is strong. Caring. Warm. Keep watching for your signs—your connection is *pure*.
- **Yellow**: Your mind is your greatest asset. Write your new beginning. Dreams really do come true.
- **Orange**: It's time to create something new. Use this creative energy to follow your bliss.
- **Red**: Your willpower is strong at this point. Be courageous and take a leap of faith.
- **Black**: You are protected during this awakening stage in your life. Don't worry. Only *love* cloaks you.

*What message is my pet sending by using a butterfly as a sign?*

When our pets choose the butterfly as their sign of choice, their message is a very beautiful one... "Yes, I'm right here. Please talk to me. Tell me how you're feeling. I can hear you. I'm right here to help ease your sorrow."

**Across the veil** into the Afterlife, *Love* is everything.

# 22

# Dragonflies

*An animal's eyes have the power to speak a
great language. ~Martin Buber*

The dragonfly also symbolizes transformation. They, too, remind us to bring more lightness and joy into our world. They carry the wisdom of change and adaptability in life.

The dragonfly can appear and disappear in the blink of an eye. It can shift colors and race through time and portals into other worlds. A very powerful messenger, the dragonfly is full of mysticism, magic, and powers of illusion.

They can move at an amazing forty-five miles per hour, can hover like a helicopter, can fly backwards like a hummingbird, and can fly straight up, down, or side to side. What's even more startling is the fact they can do all of this while flapping their wings a mere thirty times a minute.

The best part? The dragonfly does all of this with such elegance that it can easily be compared to a very graceful ballet dancer. When Michelle witnessed a dragonfly as her sign from her parrot, she marveled at its beauty.

*My day was filled with mowing grass, pulling weeds, and replacing mulch in my flower garden. As I sat on the ground, thinking of Dude, my recently deceased parrot, tears started to cover my eyes. I missed that crazy bird something awful. Dude loved to talk. Having spent a great deal of time with me, he mastered my voice, my laugh, and my words. Dude brought more joy to my life than anything ever has.*

*Sadly, when my house was burglarized weeks earlier, Dude flew at one of the intruders. When he was struck hard, Dude's neck was broken. The surveillance cameras showed everything. The thieves were caught hours later and arrested.*

*As the tears crept across my face, I continued to spread mulch throughout the garden. "I can't count the times Dude and I walked through this particular patch," I said. Just as I said that, the brightest green dragonfly landed on my shoulder. It stole my breath away and I started talking to it like I did with Dude. For two good hours that dragonfly never moved. There was no doubt in my mind that was Dude letting me know he was here with me. Now, I see green dragonflies throughout the garden. I think Dude enjoys spreading his beautiful love all across the bright and colorful flowers. ~Belinda O., Blue Springs, Alabama.*

***How do I** know if it's a sign?*

Like butterflies, dragonflies also appear when we least expect them. Whether you're taking a walk or sitting on your deck, if a dragonfly glides near you or even lands on you, do not dismiss it.

Since their appearance has garnered your attention, they show themselves for a very good reason. Judy's experience is a good example of that. When a dragonfly stuck to her finger, she knew it was a message from her devoted cat.

*A few months after we lost our longtime pal, Eddie, we welcomed two new cats who were brother and sister; Jake and Ginger. Everything Jake owned was blue and everything*

*Ginger had was pink. My beautiful Jake passed away seven years later. We were so heartbroken, as was Ginger. I felt Jake's presence many times after his death. He would often jump up on the bed and each time I would look, there would be nothing there.*

*As time went by, we decided to get another boy to keep Ginger company. I had conversed with a breeder about a boy cat she had, but she wasn't sure if he was spoken for or not. A couple of days later, on Mother's Day, my family and I were at Epcot enjoying our time together. While we walked along, my attention turned to my hand—a bright blue dragonfly was hanging onto my finger. I stopped and showed everyone and said, "This is not normal. I wonder if this means anything."*

*Right after the dragonfly flew away, my cell phone rang. It was the breeder and she said, "Happy Mother's Day, you have a new baby boy." I instantly knew the dragonfly was Jake. Since then, I often see bright blue dragonflies in my front yard. I always say, "Hi", and tell Jake how much we love him. ~Judy S., Orlando, Florida.*

**What can the** *dragonfly teach us?*

The dragonfly is one to be honored. Since they carry messages that deal with our deeper thoughts, they ask us to pay attention to our desires. Their short lives teach us to live in the moment and to live our lives to the fullest. By living in the moment we are aware of who we are, where we are, what we are doing, what we want and don't want, and we are able to make informed choices on a moment's notice. To live in the moment, allows us to live without regret.

Just like the butterfly, the dragonfly can deliver a personal message based on its color. Using the shade of the dragonfly, you can interpret a direct meaning from your pet. Here is a repeat of the symbols for colors...

*What do the colors symbolize?*

- **White**: You are divinely connected with your pet in spirit. Look at the bigger picture that is being painted for you.

- **Purple**: Signs are all around you. Trust your gut; you know the truth.

- **Blue**: It's okay to talk to your angel in spirit. Communication is key to continuing this relationship-- talk.

- **Green**: This love is strong. Caring. Warm. Keep watching for your signs—your connection is *pure*.

- **Yellow**: Your mind is your greatest asset. Write your new beginning. Dreams really do come true.

- **Orange**: It's time to create something new. Use this creative energy to follow your bliss.

- **Red**: Your willpower is strong at this point. Be courageous and take a leap of faith.

- **Black**: You are protected during this awakening stage in your life. Don't worry. Only *love* cloaks you.

*What message is my pet sending by using a dragonfly as a sign?*

When our pets choose the dragonfly as their sign of choice, their message is a loving one... "Yes, I'm here with you. Talk to me. Share everything with me for I haven't gone anywhere. **I can hear you.**"

# 23

# Air Couriers

*When I look into the eyes of an animal I do not see an animal. I see a living being. I see a friend. I feel a soul.*
*~A.D. Williams*

Air animals, our feathered friends, are amazing messengers of the sky. Their appearance is like a sparkling diamond from the heavens. There is nothing like the feeling you get when you receive a wonderful message from the other side. Whether it's from a dearly missed pet, an angel, or a loved one, the love is still the same—divine.

Closest to the heavens, air animals are symbols of strength, both physical and mental. These mysterious creatures who inhabit the skies lend the best understanding of the invisible ways of the Afterworld.

If a particular species of bird catches our attention, we are asked to be aware. Allowing their presence to give us hope and understanding, they remind us that their powerful message lies within the special moment.

There are hundreds of air messengers in our great world and entirely too many to list here. A wonderful resource I found many years ago is a book called, *Animal Speak*, by Ted Andrews. As a follower of air and animal symbols, *Animal Speak* is by far my best tool for referencing spiritual meanings and definitions. Listed below is a small record of additional bird signs that our pets can choose to use as gifts from the other side—and the message they send with each one.

- Blue Jay – You are moving into a time when you can begin to develop the innate royalty that is within you. Follow through on all things. Look for my signs. I'll show the way.

- Chicken – Take a step back and make sure you are centered in your heart. Then approach your situation from a spiritual sense and see what your next step is—if any.

- Crow – When the crow brings a message from spirit, it is a profound confirmation and symbol of *rebirth*. The crow dwells in the past, the present, and the future, all at the same time.

- Eagle – Eagles are symbols of great power, timing, and freedom. To accept the energy of this magnificent bird is to accept the new and powerful dimension coming in your life with a heightened responsibility to your spiritual growth. It's time to discover your personal power.

- Falcon – Be patient, but accurate. The opportunity is before you to take action. This will lead you to your life's purpose. Watch for my signs; I can help.

- Finch – Stop, listen, and awaken to your surroundings. Find *joy* in the now.

- Goose – New travels are on the horizon. Expect something new to happen. Keep your eyes wide open.

- Hawk – The hawk's broad vision allows them to see what the future holds. They signify joining together with all that is. Bringing communications from the spirit world, the hawk is a superior messenger.

- Mockingbird – Look for opportunities to sing forth your own song. Follow your own path. Take what you can and apply your creative imagination and intuition in the tune that is most harmonious for you and your life.

- Owl – Darkness is of no obstacle. You have enough light inside of you to see through the illusion. Trust your intuition.

- Peacock – Acknowledge your dreams and aspirations. You have greater vision and wisdom now. Stand out and be noticed. Let your true colors shine.

- Pelican – Are you trying to store what shouldn't be saved? Free yourself from that which holds you down. Take it easy even in the most of hectic times and savor each special moment. Relax.

- Pigeon – A symbol for a time or a need to return to the security of home, the pigeon teaches you how to find your way back if you've become lost. Home is where your heart is.

- Swan – You are very sensitive. Take the time to look and really notice what is before you. Allow your inner grace to shine so that others can see it.

- Turkey – The turkey has a long history of association with spirituality and the honoring of Mother Earth. When the turkey crosses your path, you have been gifted with the blessings you receive every day. Give thanks.

- Woodpecker – Follow your own unique rhythm and flight. Do what works for you in the manner best for you. The door is wide open; it's safe to follow your dreams. Trust that your angel is guiding you the entire way.

- Vulture – The vulture soars with Grace and Ease. When this bird crosses your path, you are told you'll be noticed for what you do, rather than for how you appear.

**Signs from the** Afterlife are created from the heart center of our loyal companions. If an air messenger touches you and hugs your heart, then it is a sign. Many may argue that following signs from spirit animals is insane, and that's okay. The only thing that matters is your own development and your personal discernment into the messages you receive.

This is your journey and yours alone, and no one can take that away. Nancy's experience is a wonderful example of how to build a stronger connection by learning *spirit language.*

*Jessie came into my life as a beautiful calico kitten. She purred in my ear when I asked for divine guidance in choosing her from a litter of five. When it became obvious that Jessie was spending her last days with me, I struggled with playing God and sending her to Heaven. Upon returning from the vet, my family and I were sitting in the living room talking about how Jessie was a blessing in our lives when we heard a kitten meowing. I ran to the door certain I would find a cat on the stairs but to my surprise, I found a beautiful yellow finch sitting on the power wire chirping. I am certain it was Jessie confirming she was safe on the other side of the Rainbow Bridge. I am eternally grateful for her sign and for her thirteen years with me. ~Nancy R., Minneapolis, Minnesota.*

**Air animals share** amazing messages from the spiritual realm. Our beloved pets let us know in no uncertain terms… "I am here, kissing you from Heaven. Feel my energy and allow me to lift your spirit. Never forget how much I love you."

# 24

# Land & Sea Messengers

*The time will come when men such as I will look upon the
murder of animals as now they look upon the murder of men.*
*~Leonardo Da Vinci*

Animals are supremely spiritual beings. We as humans
have long overlooked this. When we are able to make
the connection that animals are a part of us and a piece of the
greater cosmic fabric that makes up our lives, then we can truly
begin to learn more about the world around us and the world
within us.

When we start to believe in animals as spiritual teachers
and messengers, it opens up a whole new dimension within our
lives. Animals suddenly become more than simple pets or
companions. They become holders of ancient wisdom and
carriers of divine guidance. They school us on our journeys and
nourish us on all levels (physically, mentally, and spiritually)
to help us sustain life, and maintain balance with nature.

An animal symbol can bring us a message in several ways.
We can physically cross paths with it, we can dream about
them, they can visit us in our meditations, or we can even have
them as pets. Totem animals, or creatures we feel a very strong
connection to, can and do influence our lives.

Each animal is unique in what they represent spiritually

and physically. Their communications are given out of love and their wisdom is here to teach us more about ourselves. We each have so much more to discover about life and life after death. By incorporating animal messages into our lives, they can help establish our spiritual goals.

As we begin to engage with our Animal Totems, (also known as Power Animals, Spirit Animals, and Animal Guides), we will start to recognize the synchronicities. We will want to understand the secret messages that are hidden in plain sight all around us. We will start to notice that signs and signals are everywhere.

*What can Animal Totems teach us?*

Animal Totems show us how to find the wisdom and meaning in the symbolic realms of spirit beings. Their inspiring messages bring remarkable insight into what we're going through at the moment we acknowledge them.

*What message is my pet sending by using an Animal Totem as a sign?*

When our pets place Animal Totems along our path, they're not only letting us know they're with us, they are also giving us a uniquely choreographed message. They tell us, "Love is in the air and to show you how much I love you, here is my symbol for you."

**Signs from our** pets in the Afterlife are filled with *love*. If the messenger embraces our hearts, then it is a sign.

There are too many animal guides to list here. As a second reminder, a wonderful book to have in your possession is by Ted Andrews called, *Animal Speak*. As a follower of air and animal signs, this book is by far my best tool for referencing their spiritual assistance. Another great source to research additional information is located at a website called, *Spirit Animal Totems;* www.spirit-animals.com.

No Animal Symbol should be dismissed. Here is a short list of Animal Symbols that our pets can use as Gifts from the other side. Remember, they are the ones choosing the type of communication to share:

- Alligator – The keeper and protector of all knowledge, the alligator reminds you that patience is key right now. Breathe. And give yourself time to make those changes.

- Badger – This is a new opportunity to develop self-expression. Have faith in yourself and your abilities. Tell a new story about yourself and your life. Walk your own path at your own pace.

- Bat – Indicates initiation; a new beginning that brings promise and power after the change. Pay attention to the signs around you, (physical, mental, emotional, and spiritual), and follow through on new ideas.

- Bear – Go within to awaken your power. Delve deep into your heart to find the significance of your journey and bring it out into the open. Taste the honey of life.

- Beaver – A symbol for never giving up, the beaver carries great foresight and is a true visionary. Act now on your dreams to make them a reality.

- Cat – Trust your intuition. It's time to believe in yourself. The cat informs you that you have everything you need in your life, right now, to make your dreams come true.

- Coyote – Creator, teacher, and keeper of magic, the coyote reminds you not to become too serious. Old rules no longer apply; anything is possible.

- Chipmunk – Synchronicity is in the air when we see the chipmunk. Teaching us that Spirit is always close, the chipmunk encourages us to ask for help and guidance. Now is a perfect time to ask for a sign. Believe in magic.

- Deer – New opportunities will open doors to adventure. Be gentle with yourself and seek your inner treasures. Lead by doing and showing the way.

- Dolphin – Breathe new life into yourself. Listen to your intuition. Be open to new experiences. Get out, play, and explore. Enjoy the moment for it shall not pass this way again.

- Dog – The energy of the dog is always reminding you to be loyal and truthful to yourself. It is important to love yourself in order to be of assistance to others.

- Elephant – Embodying strength and power, the elephant reminds you what your life's driving force is about and then gives you the desire to pursue it. Prepare to draw upon the most ancient of wisdom and power. Elephants share their dreams and help you explore new possibilities not yet considered.

- Fox – Holding the magic of pure luck, the fox brings the energies of opportunity. Any prize can fall to you. You have all the tools and resources needed to turn money, career, or living difficulties, around.

- Frog – Your real value is the value of the you that is within. Symbolizing transformation, the frog reminds you to try and be very patient with your awakening.

- Goat – This is the time to begin new endeavors. The goat

holds the knowledge of how to stretch and reach new heights and goals.

- Horse – With souls riding into and out of the worlds upon it, the horse is closely tied with new beginnings. Teaching you how to ride into new directions to awaken your personal freedom and power, the horse brings with it new journeys.

- Lion – A symbol of the sun and of gold, the lion awakens you to new energies. Trust your intuition and imagination. These will add new sunshine to your life. The ultimate protector of the home, the lion reminds you to be bold, be wise, and be fierce.

- Monkey – Things aren't always how they seem. Use your sixth sense to find your truth.

- Pig – Stop your procrastinating ways and get organized. Changes are coming; they're on the horizon.

- Rabbit – The Rabbit shows you how to notice the signs around you. They can help you recognize the tides of movement in your life, and can enable you to become even more creative in your world.

- Raccoon – Take the time to look at the whole picture. The seen and the unseen. The raccoon reminds you to leave no stone unturned in your search for answers.

- Skunk – Examine your self-image. People are going to notice you. Walking your talk is the only way to respect yourself and your beliefs. The skunk doesn't need to spray to be powerful. Protect yourself without speaking a word.

- Snake – Your transformation is natural and normal. Set

your intentions clearly. Change is good. Know that you are safe and have nothing to fear.

- Squirrel – Masters at preparing, the squirrel reminds us always to make time to socialize and play. Have more fun and don't take life so seriously.

- Tiger – As the ruler of the Earth and its energies, the tiger awakens new passion and the power within life. New adventures will manifest. Make a move to your dreams and goals; use care and quietness as your tools.

- Turtle – A symbol for mother Earth and for longevity, the turtle reminds you to get connected with your primal essence, your soul. It's time to recognize the abundance before you and take your time allowing the flow to work for you instead of against you. Everything you need is available to you if you approach it in the right manner and time... slow and steady wins the race.

- Whale – An ancient symbol for creation—be it of the body or the world—the whale reminds us to honor our soul's purpose. Claim the destiny that you know is yours. Embrace the unknown.

- Wolf – Representing the spirit of freedom, the wolf reminds you to take a new path, take a new journey. You are safe and protected at all times. You are the governor of your life; create it and it is yours.

**Signs from our** pets in the Afterlife are filled with *love*. If the messenger hugs your heart, then *it is a sign*.

# Part Four

## For Your Soul

# 25

# Ask and Ye Shall Receive

*The best and most beautiful things in the world
cannot be seen or even touched. They must be felt
with the heart. ~Helen Keller*

W hen something happens that stops us in our tracks and makes us question why it happened, it may be a sign from our pets. Don't dismiss anything. Most of us have been trained to believe in only what our eyes perceive, and not in what we feel, sense, or hear. Just because spirit cannot be seen, that doesn't mean they're not with us. One of the biggest reasons we miss seeing the beauty of the Afterlife, is due to our inability to *believe* in the gifts they share. It's not a secret anymore. Our blessed pets really do want to communicate with us.

There is **NO** one *Sign* that fits all. If we can think it, so can they. If your pet has a certain sign that appears over and over again, then that's their way of contacting you. The only thing to remember is that *it's your sign* and it belongs only to you. Maureen's story is a wonderful example of how to build a stronger connection by learning a new language. Her dog in spirit, Chance, validates their remarkable love.

*During a weekend nature retreat, my friends and I headed to Baker River to sleuth around with a metal detector. In one spot I was drawn to, we pulled up a rusted end clasp to a leash.*

*Unsuccessful in trying to figure out the word for that piece, we dug again ten feet up the hill. This time we found a rusted cast iron St. Bernard piggy bank. My friend suggested that the two finds were a sign for me to get a new dog. I had recently lost the love of my life, my pit bull named, Chance. Together, we spent fifteen amazing years.*

*The next morning our first assignment was to reflect in silence what we experienced over the weekend. So I took the opportunity to channel, Chance. Her message was remarkable. "Let go of the leash, open that clip up, and let go of the leash." I found it interesting she called the piece on the leash a **clip**. It was a very emotional experience for me. Yet, I knew she was right. I needed to move on and let myself find love again. The first anniversary of her death was fast approaching and I missed her badly.*

*We immediately went online to the American Welfare Society Shelter for animals and found a picture of an eight-year-old white shepherd named, Meah.*

*Meah was a gentle giant who was calm and very loving. Someone in the shelter described her as being elegant and in a matter of seconds I fell in love and agreed to adopt her. On our way home, my friend asked if I was going to change her name. I told her I would feel bad if I was fifty-six years old and someone did that to me. At that very second, a car went by with a license plate that read, "YESIREE." Talk about confirmation. The greatest validation I received however, came when I realized I had adopted Meah on Pet Memorial Day. How fitting that Chance came through to honor her presence in my life. I am very blessed. ~Maureen M., Windham, Maine.*

**It is okay** to ask your pet in the afterworld for a message.

Especially if you're just learning how to speak the *language of spirit*. In order to gain confidence, we can ask for a specific sign to not only help us understand they are with us, but to assist us in learning what to recognize.

At first, we want to make it something simple. For example, we might ask for a special song, a shiny penny, a wild deer, a white butterfly, a green Jeep; anything we want actually. Once we choose our sign, we can then walk outside and gaze up into the sky. We can tell our beloved companions about the sign we've chosen for them, and for us, and then we might say something like this… "When I see this sign from you, I promise to acknowledge it, and you, too."

No matter the way our sign appears, whether it's on television, on a billboard we pass by, on the internet, in a magazine, on a T-shirt… **it is our sign**. We give big thanks and then delight in the fact that we're now speaking our pet's language; *Spirit Language*. Then, we can do it all over again. Asking for a sign and believing in it when it's delivered can help in relieving dark grief. It won't take it away by any means, but it can help us to understand that just because our pets shed their physical bodies, it doesn't mean they stop loving those they leave behind.

We will all meet again and when that time comes, it will be a grand and very special reunion. Until then, it is perfectly normal to continue our relationships with our pets in spirit. Let's take Angela's messages for example. It is quite remarkable how one sign can lead into another, and then another. Angela's task was to put all the pieces together.

*Winston, my handsome Rhodesian Ridgeback, was the love of my life. After he passed away, a friend recommended the* book, *"The Secret"*, by Rhonda Byrne. She wanted me to understand how our souls live on and how everything is made up of energy.

I found Lyn Ragan's book, *"Wake Me Up! Love and The Afterlife."* In it, she made a comment about devoting all of her time learning as much as she could regarding the Afterlife. I smiled because that is exactly what I am doing right now.

During my lunch hour, I drove into town and started to practice the law-of-attraction for a parking space. It worked. I found a large spot and pulled right in. As I walked back from the ticket machine, I had to stop dead in my tracks because the building I parked in front of was called, *"The Secret Treatment Rooms"*. This instantly reminded me of my book, The Secret. Now, I'm new to this, but surely that had to be a sign.

I then proceeded in and out of various shops, but in one of the charity shops I saw a book in the middle of the shelf titled, *"No Greater Love."* It was the ONLY book turned with the cover showing; all the rest had their spines on show. Two books down from that one, I noticed the title of another book called, *"The Best of Me."*

By this time, I knew they were ALL signs from my gorgeous boy, Winston. He was leading the way, still, and was asking only one thing from me— to trust, to believe, and to receive his divine love. ~Angela T., Harrogate, North Yorkshire.

There is *NO* one Sign that fits all. It's okay to ask for a sign… ask and ye shall receive.

**Trust. Believe. Receive.**

# Acknowledgments

An enormous thank you to everyone who graciously shared their amazing Afterlife experiences with their beloved pets: Marley B., Rickie F., Teresa C., Janet M., Helen B., Judy S., Regina B., Penny W., Diane B., Betty B., Linda W., Dorothy L., Nancy S., Rachel G., Denise O., Becky N., Mack B., Melissa P., Robin T., Sandy R., Belinda O., Lynn P., Pamela K., Angela T., Nancy R. Marilyn B., Sunny W., Donna J., Marti T., Lynda M., Ethel B., Laura P., Missy R., Lisa M., Kim W., Nicole B., Jake E., Anne F., Dixie M., Paige D., Brandi M., Monica D., Tina C., BettyJane H., Beverly W., Melinda O., Judy S., and Maureen M. Without you and your beautiful fur-kids, this book would not be complete. I am forever grateful.

A big thank you for her amazing talent and beautiful heart; my editor and friend, Marley Gibson Burns. To all of my family here in the physical world, and to all of my family and dear friends on the other side, ***thank you*** for loving me. To my Angels and Guides, I am eternally *addicted* to your Love.

And to the one my heart belongs, Chip Oney. My gratitude for your remarkable guidance and unconditional Love is greater than us both.

# Resources

1. *Animal-Speak: The Spiritual & Magical Powers of Creatures Great & Small*, by Ted Andrews.

2. *Signs From The Afterlife: Identifying Gifts From The Other Side*, by Author, Lyn Ragan

3. Joanne Walmsley, creator of: *sacredscribesangelnumbers.blogspot.com*

4. *Angel Numbers 101: The Meaning of 111, 123, 444, and Other Number Sequences*, by Doreen Virtue.

5. *Spirit Animal Totems and The Messages They Bring You;* www.spirit-animals.com.

6. *Spirit Animal—The Ultimate Guide;* www.spiritanimal.info

7. *Learn About Nature* at www.learnaboutnature.com

8. Pure Spirit at www.pure-spirit.com

9. Brent Atwater, Author, *Animal Reincarnation: Everything You Always Wanted to Know*

10. Quotes by, Anthony Douglas Williams—*Inside the Divine Pattern.*

# About The Author

Photo: Christopher Yenom

Lyn Ragan knew at the age of fourteen that she would write a book one day. She subscribed to *True Crime* and *True Detective*, reading each edition faithfully while plotting her fiction novel she never wrote. Twenty-five years later, she met the love of her life never thinking she'd be involved in a real-life crime. After her fiancée's murder, she followed his guidance by way of ADC's, (After Death Communications). From the other side, Chip insisted she write their story. Following her struggles with grief and added defiance, she reluctantly gave in and penned their first two books, *Wake Me Up! Love and The Afterlife*, and, *We Need To Talk: Living With The Afterlife*. While writing her first novel, Lyn was introduced to the spiritual arts of energy work. She pursued meditation faithfully and went on to study Reiki Healing, Aura Energy, and Chakra Balancing. She later used her studies to become a professional Aura Photographer, an Ordained Minister, a children's book author, a publisher, and later, wrote her third book, *Signs From The Afterlife*. Lyn enjoys sharing Chip's afterlife communications and hopes their story sheds new light on continuing relationships with loved ones passed. She lives in Atlanta with her fur-kids, Scooby, Chipper, Dusty, and Scooter.

Lyn can be found online at *www.LynRagan.com* and on Facebook at *SignsFromPetsInTheAfterlife*.

Made in the USA
Middletown, DE
28 July 2019